I'D RATHER TALK TO DEAD PEOPLE

MY JOURNEY AS A PARANORMAL RESEARCHER

KITSIE DUNCAN

BEYOND THE FRAY

Publishing

ISBN 13: 978-1-7344198-8-7

Beyond The Fray Publishing, a division of Beyond The Fray, LLC, San Diego, CA

www.beyondthefraypublishing.com

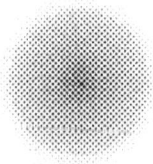

BEYOND THE FRAY

Publishing

To my dad for being my inspiration, my husband for putting up with me,
and my crew, Carter and Clayton, for always being down to hang out in the
dark.

I'm Kitsie Duncan, and I've been investigating the paranormal for twelve years. I guess you could say I'm a late bloomer. I didn't even open myself up to the paranormal until I was in my late thirties. I was terrified of even the thought of ghosts or spirits as a kid, this fear followed me into my adult life. So, what does this mean? Well, it means I don't have that story where I saw a ghost as a child, then spent the rest of my life proving it was real. Even though I grew up in the house all the other kids in the neighborhood called haunted, I never saw anything. You know how every neighborhood has that one house they call the haunted house, well, that was my house, I came to find that out in my high school days.

In my early teens, things would go missing in the house all the time, only to show back up a day or two later, where we knew we had left it, and where we had searched for it numerous times. It was the running joke of the house. If something went missing, my mother would say, "Give it a couple of days, the ghost took it, and he'll bring it back."

Now I'm not gonna lie, there were creepy vibes there from time to time, but my mom would just say it was my overactive imagination and thank God she did. I shut it all out, being terrified of anything paranormal at the time (thanks to the movie *Poltergeist*).

I can still remember the day my friend told me what was so obvious now as I think back on it. I was a teenager when a friend finally set me down and told me that my house was the neighborhood haunted house. I played it off like he was kidding. But the serious look upon his face told me he wasn't joking. He pointed to a window and told me about the time he had seen a ghost there. He was the local paperboy and upon his route he'd looked up and seen a white face holding a candle. Outside the fact that he was serious, and I now believed him, what made his story even more frightening was the room he was pointing to was MY BEDROOM.

A few years later when I was a senior in high school, I had a friend spend the night, and we decided to go to the local Toys "R" Us and buy a Ouija board, because that was what girls did in the '80s. My parents were at one of my little sister's softball games, so we took it out on the back deck, thinking nothing would happen, but something did happen. It moved and answered all our questions. Now you'd think we'd be scared, but I wasn't, in fact we laughed more than anything. We kept playing with it until my parents and sisters returned home. Not wanting them to see what we'd been doing, we put the board in my room and thought nothing of the fact that one needs to close the Ouija board session; something I learned about years later.

That night, we went to bed late, but sometime around five in the morning, I was awoken out of a deep sleep by a gruff and loud male voice saying right in my ear, "GET OUT!"

I woke up my friend, told her what had happened, then raced out of the house, Ouija board in hand, and into her little hatchback, with plans to destroy the board. At this time, there were rumors going around the school that you can't burn a Ouija board, so we didn't try that. Instead, we went to some quiet road and tried to break it by running over it with her car. It was quite comical, looking back. But the planchette wouldn't break. We finally gave up and returned to my house before my parents woke up, and just threw it in the trash.

The odd and sometimes scary things continued but soon waned then eventually stopped. I quickly put it out of my mind and blamed it on the overactive imagination my mother was always telling me I had.

Let's fast forward years. I'm married to my high school boyfriend and after spending time living abroad in Germany while he was in the military, we return to our hometown. He gets a job working at my dad's steel plant and I'm working as a sales executive. Our marriage up to this point was amazing until we moved in to my parent's house. We were wanting to buy a house, and this was a way to save money. Now it might have been because we married young, or because we moved back to our hometown, but things in our relationship got DARK and fast. He started drinking, and things got a bit physical too. My work started to suffer, and it was hard to pay our bills.

I can still recall this one night like it was yesterday. My six-month-old son was colicky, and I was trying to let him cry himself to sleep. This was back when baby monitors were new and only audio. As I was listening to my son cry, , I heard the same voice from my teen years say loudly, "Shut up!" I raced back to the room, picked up my son and exited quickly.

Whatever had been there from my teen years was still there. But why? Maybe the spirit didn't like that I had returned home or maybe it didn't like me and my ex being together. Whatever the reason, it was evident it didn't' like my son crying.

In 1999 the man who raised me since I was nine years old died suddenly from a massive heart attack. He was legally my stepfather, but to me he was Daddy. There were no goodbyes. It happened one night when the world was asleep, and that night shook me and my family to the core.

I'm not a religious person. I believe that if you do good things, good things come to you. However, I had always believed in ghosts, spirits and entities. I just didn't know anything about them, because they were terrifying to me. Then my dad passed. It was then I needed to know more.

I felt his presence from time to time, and I wasn't scared (well, AS scared). He was so young, only fifty-three, just three years older than I am now. He died so suddenly, and there were no goodbyes, and for me it was almost impossible to get closure. And I needed that. So I started to open my mind up to the paranormal. I found a paranormal investigative series on cable and watched several episodes, and then another series, and another. And somehow in my mind, this made things less scary for me. Nobody investigating was dying, nobody was being seriously hurt, and everything that scared me about the paranormal wasn't even really a thing.

So, I drank in every paranormal series on TV, did research, and learned about the paranormal investigative equipment, researched techniques that weren't on the TV shows, watching documentaries, etc., etc. And then I met a couple who was a part of a paranormal team here in Indiana. They asked me to join them on an investigation, and I jumped at the chance.

I was so pumped. The location had been on one of

the ghost shows I was obsessed with. The stories that were told about the location were legendary: a little girl named Rachel, and a doctor who treated smallpox patients, with some of those patients dying on the premises. I was beyond excited. There were probably fifteen of us in the group. I had my brand-new video camera that took video in the dark. I was terrified and ridiculously excited all at once, until we walked in. We were given a tour by the man who set up the paranormal investigations, and he left us there for the rest of the night. I was the new kid, so I just sat back and watched for the most part, while taking video the whole time. But I wasn't scared anymore, I wasn't anxious, and I almost felt at home in the notoriously haunted location.

The group I was with was intense, constantly provoking, one guy even yelled into the darkness, "Come at me, bro." And that was when I knew this wasn't the kind of investigation for me. Another member of the team claimed to be scratched; no one was around when it allegedly happened. So, I silently questioned if it was paranormal or self-inflicted. What I did know was that I wasn't scared. I somehow knew there was nothing bad here, and I felt like I was living one of those crazy overdramatic cable shows I had binged so hard on. And NO ONE needs extra drama in their life, especially the self-created type. I left that place wondering if this was even for me.

But they say everything happens for a reason. I went

with that team to one final location, and it was at that location that I knew I was hooked and was informed that I am sensitive to the paranormal. Wait, what?! Yep. I was on the tour, and one of the people giving the tour was a medium named Teresa Lynch, and after feeling like I was going to pass out for no apparent reason while walking down the hallway of a now empty elementary school, having to sit down right there (I thought I might be dying). After Teresa found out I was okay, she asked me if I was an empath. I in turn looked at her like she was crazy. She then let me know that I had just walked through a portal, and it affects people with empathic abilities. My mind was in overdrive the rest of the evening during the investigation. Was she right? I had no idea how right she was.

That was my last investigation with that team, but certainly not my last investigation. I was heading out of town for work to Virginia Beach, and a friend of mine told me about Ferry Plantation. So, I set up an overnight investigation while I was there, took what little equipment I had at the time, and hoped to hell I knew what I was doing. Ferry Planation is a gorgeous home that is now set up as a museum by the Friends of Ferry Plantation.

The house was amazing, and the ladies who took myself and my husband, Chris, on the tour were so informative and loved the house with all that they had. We took the tour, found out all the paranormal hot spots, and went on with my very first investigation with me as the lead. In case you haven't noticed, I like to jump into things headfirst and worry about it later.

We captured some amazing evidence that I still to this day can't explain. But as we were about to finish up for the night, I rounded the corner with my Sony green screen video camera in hand, which was unfortunately pointed straight toward the ground, and I saw my very first ghost apparition. I was floored. I was coming out of the parlor into the living room, looked into a doorway, and saw a little girl that was all grayish, but I could see every detail of her long curly hair, her tiny little ankle-length dress, and her pinafore. Half of her body was blocked by the doorway, but I saw her sweet little head peek farther around the door, make eye contact with me, smile at me with the sweetest smile, and then she backed herself behind the corner of the doorway, and I assumed she went down a hallway. I rushed to go to her. I wasn't scared at all, I wanted to talk to her, but when I made my way around that same doorway, there was no hallway she could have gone down. There was a doorway out that was locked and sealed shut, and there was a table in front of it. I mean, WHAAAT?!

I told my husband immediately, and his first words were, "If you didn't get it on video, it didn't happen." He did have a point, and the saying still holds on every investigation I've done since. However, after we were finished investigating for the night, I asked the ladies who had given us the tour of the building if anyone else had seen what I just saw. They proceeded to pull out a scrapbook with several drawings of what others had seen and some actual photos of the exact little girl I had seen. In the exact same dress, with the exact same curly hair, and even one of those photos portrayed the exact same smile I had seen her give me. I could not believe it. Maybe Teresa was onto something. No one else had seen her in our group. My friend Amanda was along for the investigation and had been walking in front of me, with my husband behind me. I was starting to think maybe I was sensitive to the paranormal.

And at this point you could say I was obsessed with the paranormal. I wanted to know all the things about it and find out more about this, what I call my "crazy" (because I have no scientific proof behind some things I experience), and why was I so afraid of this paranormal world my whole life? I literally blame the 1980s Poltergeist franchise for this.

I booked all the investigations and brought friends and my husband with me along the way. The investigations took me to some incredible locations where I met amazing people and learned a lot about myself. I've met other empaths and talented mediums, who have helped me grow and learn to accept this newfound superpower I never knew I had.

When I started inviting some friends along, we would film our adventures, and I would edit them together with horrible audio and grainy footage, and people on the internet watched, and most of the people who watched liked what they were seeing, so I kept at it.

It was always a fun way to hang out with friends. And we did things this way for years, and I decided it was time to get serious, to focus on the evidence and how I was getting it. So I narrowed the team down to myself and two others, and the evidence was so compelling that I ended up submitting our final edited investigations to Prime Video, Amazon accepted our show *Oddity Files*, and we gained a following there. Then Clayton and I started a podcast called, again, *Oddity Files*, and we gained another following there. And now I've been asked to write a book. This journey has been nothing short of amazing for me. And I thank you for being a part of this journey. Whether you're a longtime follower or someone gave you this book as a gift, I appreciate you being here.

So now that you know a little about me and why I am obsessed with this paranormal journey I've decided to take, what you are about to read are some of the most emotional, profound, and mind-blowing investigations I've been on during this journey. I've learned ghosts aren't scary; if you treat them with respect, they will do the same. I've never run into a demon on any investigation, and I have loads of theories on all the paranormal things, so sit back, pour yourself your favorite beverage, and let's go ghost hunting, shall we?

CHAPTER 1

CULBERTSON MANSION

*A*fter several years into my paranormal obsession, I narrowed the team down to just myself, my son Carter, and friend of the family, Clayton. Our combined energies coupled with our mutual respect for the paranormal has made it possible to get the evidence we have over the years. I'm a sensitive/empath who searches for evidence to confirm what I'm feeling, hearing, and seeing. Clayton is a skeptic who is open minded, and at this point, this was only Carter's third paranormal investigation.

I was one of the first people to be able to investigate the Culbertson Mansion State Historic Site. Thankfully, my friend Belinda Collins was able to get me and my team in for a night. The dandelion-yellow house is stunning. Just pulling up in the daylight hours, I was in awe.

It was built in 1867 for the richest man in America at the time, Robert Culbertson.

As you can imagine, no expense was spared. I could go on and on about details such as the hand-carved wooden staircase and the elaborate fabric wallpaper, but I know you're here for the good stuff. The hauntings. Going into the location, I didn't have a lot to go on for the paranormal side of things. I was told by my friend that her husband had had an experience with a woman in a green dress. So I met with Gary Collins so he could tell me his story. The story was simple, just a woman in a green Victorian dress seen within the home. No real interaction was had with her at the time, which didn't leave me with much to go on.

This was our first investigation with the coolest piece of equipment I have ever owned, the Odd Box. My wonderful husband had gotten it for me for Christmas the previous year, and I had spent months and months learning about it and learning how to use it. I had gone against my cardinal rule of not investigating or using any paranormal equipment in my house to fine-tune this amplifier speaker with crystals and copper wire, all meant to lend any paranormal activity extra energy conductors and protection for anyone using the device. It also has a large brick exterior battery, which I always encourage spirits to draw energy from, because it has that much power in it. There are two ways to use this device: you can hook it up to a spirit box, ghost box or anything of the like, or to one of the many apps available for tablets and iPads, and fine-tune the sound to your liking. My favorite part is the reverb the box has available. It makes things a little creepier, and honestly for me, it makes it easier to understand.

While learning to use the device, I had many interesting conversations with people I believed to be spirits. My mind was blown away. However, about a week before our trip to the Culbertson mansion, I had gotten it out to show a friend. And instantly we had responses, and just on a whim, I asked about our upcoming investigation, and the name Anna came over. She sounded young, I would have to guess around the age of ten to fourteen. And that was it, nothing after that. I pretty much played it off to coincidence, and that was it. Let's get back to the investigation at hand.

The crew started bringing in the equipment, and we came up with a game plan. So much ground to cover in so little time is usually the name of the game when we are investigating. We did a quick tour of the house to get the lay of the land. And we chose to start on the top floor of the house in the children's playroom. It was set up with half as a museum with showcases full of information on the Culbertsons, and the other half was set up as a playroom. We set our equipment up in the playroom section.

We'd brought with us a set of dowsing rods, which are an old-school way to communicate with spirits.

They are L-shaped metal rods that are easily purchased online. It's said that these rods react to energy. I feel they are an easy way for a spirit to manipulate the rods' positions in order to answer yes or no questions, or sometimes communicate with them in more ways than even that. We brought up a spirit box, which is a hand-held AM/FM radio that can very quickly scan through radio stations. So fast, that if it were to pick up a radio station, it would move on so quickly you wouldn't even hear more than one syllable. And we attached our spirit box to the Odd Box. An Ovilus, which is a device with a large database of words that by sensing the electro-magnetic energy of the room and temperature, it's said that spirits can manipulate the energy and use this to tell investigators what they want to say. This specific piece of equipment is something we rarely have luck with; however, we do use it from time to time. And of course, some infrared light cameras that can see in the dark.

I start every investigation in any room in the place we are investigating by saying out loud to any spirits that might be within earshot that I am not there to hurt them, harm them, or take them away from their home. I make it noticeably clear that myself and anyone I brought with me are surrounded by love, light, peace, and positivity, and we're only there to talk to spirits who are of the same energy. I introduce myself and my team, and I tell them we just want to know their story. I so desperately want to know their story, that's why I do this.

We all settled in for the round. Since this place wasn't regularly investigated, there weren't seats set up for people to relax in as they seek communication with the other side. So, we found our spots within the space available. I got down on the kids' level and sat cross-legged on the floor, not sure if it would help them relate to me or not, but it was worth a shot.

We started with a quick EVP burst session. EVP stands for electronic voice phenomenon. Generally we don't have a lot of luck with EVPs on a handheld digital voice recorder (I literally bought mine at a pawnshop, the worse the quality of audio, the easier it is to help pick up disembodied voices), and this was one of those times. I did personally hear the voice of a child, and sadly no one else in the group did. This is something that happens often; I hear a voice, the crew doesn't.

Sometimes I just feel the energy, and sometimes that energy has a gender to it, an age range, and sometimes a name. I call it my "crazy"; many others call it being an empath or medium. It's a really cool superpower I still don't have all the answers to. But what is so amazing about this to me is that often the evidence backs up these "feelings" or "energies" I am picking up on. I explore it as often as I can. Now, there is no proof to back up "feelings," and yes, I know that, and I never take what I am feeling as the only evidence. But I blurt out what I feel and hope the evidence of the investigation will back it up, and then my "crazy" ends up enhancing the story or even just filling in the blanks. I am still learning about it every time we investigate.

My "crazy" was telling me I heard a young girl. I couldn't make out what the voice said, but it was a great start. Sadly, the voice was not picked up on the voice recorder. And then it came back to me, the Odd Box communication I'd had the week before. I decided the dowsing rods might be the easiest way to communicate with the spirit, who was not really used to the modern forms of investigative equipment.

And whatever spirit we were communicating with figured these out very quickly, which was unexpected and so exciting. Heart racing, I began a quick Q&A session, asking only yes or no questions, and the energy would cross the rods for a yes answer and leave them straight out for a no answer. In between, the rods are reset to straight out.

The first question I asked was if the entity was a female, thinking this might be the voice of Anna, and they crossed very slowly into a perfect X. After the female spirit uncrossed them for me upon command, I tried to find out the age of the spirit. I next asked if the spirit was under the age of eighteen, and they crossed perfectly and faster than the first time, a yes answer. And at the same time, the Ovilus said its first and only relevant word of the evening, "FIFTEEN," so I immediately asked our guest if she was fifteen years old, and the rods crossed immediately. Upon asking her to uncross the rods so I could ask her another question, they uncrossed hard and fast.

Trying desperately to find out who we were communicating with, with only yes or no answers, I asked if she had died in the house, and they crossed immediately again. We had known that none of the Culbertsons' children had died in the house, nor had any of the consecutive owners, so we had a true mystery on our hands. On a whim, and because I'm crazy, I asked if her name was Anna, and they crossed immediately again. I asked her some more questions, and we found out she was the only one in the room who was not alive, and that she was having fun communicating, which broke my heart a little.

Just then a noise was heard in the hallway just off the playroom, and immediately the mood changed as Clayton saw a shadow creep across the ceiling of that hallway. We were all completely confused at this point. Anna had just told us she was the only spirit in the room with us. Which was something I've never understood. In my experience, some spirits are able to see and interact with other spirits, yet this one didn't seem to be able to, or could she?

While Clayton went out to investigate the hallway, I tried to keep the lines of communication open with Anna. Just then, the rods quickly turned at the same time toward the side of the room opposite the hallway. I then started to sense that this young girl was scared. She immediately confirmed this by crossing the rods after I asked her, and I told her that Clayton would take care of it, and that she could stay with us, and that I would protect her. She then went on to tell us that the shadow in the hallway was a nanny. My next thought was to turn on the spirit box attached to the Odd Box to see if Anna could communicate with us more directly. For me, sometimes just yes and no answers aren't enough, and this was one of those times.

Upon setting up and firing up the spirit box and the Odd Box, I like to explain the device to each spirit we encounter, so I did so and asked specifically to speak to Anna. A young female voice came over almost immediately, saying hello. The next thing that came through was the exact same voice as the girl who said hello, saying the name Anna. ARE YOU KIDDING ME?! We then asked what the nanny's name was, and the words "sister" and then "Anna" came over at once. Our minds were blown, and I was so excited to see this device in action at an actual haunted location. I was sure to let Anna know what an amazing job she was doing and encouraged her to communicate with us more.

I was curious if the nanny/sister had left, because her answers were forthcoming, and she, the same voice that had answered all of my other questions, didn't seem afraid anymore. I asked her if we were now alone, and she came over again and said, "Yes." Eager to learn more, Clayton then asked what the maid's name was, and the name Anna came over again in the same voice. Was Anna a maid, and her sister the nanny? Why did the nanny not want her to speak to us? The next thing to come over were these words and phrases in this order: "I love you," "Anna," and "Listen." And then she asked, "You hear me?" The first two phrases came over AGAIN in the exact same voice that we now knew was Anna, but the word "listen" was not. It sounded male and stern. Then before we could even contemplate where the male voice came from, Anna asked us, "You hear me?" I can't lie, this got me a little teary eyed. In all my years of investigating, I had never had a complete real-time conversation with a spirit, and to me the fact that Anna asked if I could hear her meant she was having the same feelings of amazement and joy.

It was amazing, we could hear her, and she was confirming the fact that she could hear us. There is no greater feeling as a paranormal investigator than when your thoughts and evidence are all completely backed up by the spirits themselves. We continued our questions, and next we asked where her family was.

Just then, Carter, who had been steadily behind the camera, felt something touching his arm. He was in the middle of the room, and none of the crew was within five feet of him, and we asked the Wonder Box if someone was touching Carter's arm. And immediately a voice of an even younger child, possibly a male, said, "I am."

I got an overwhelming feeling of several energies all entering our space at once, and it was felt by the entire team. When the team feels the same thing I do, it's always an amazing moment. There was no sense of dread or mal intent, it just felt like they were there to see what we were up to, and to see what all the noise was coming from the Wonder Box. Were other spirits of the location ready to speak with us as well? Was the male spirit who said listen summoning everyone to where we were?

We then turn our questioning to the spirit who was closest to Carter and had touched him. I asked who had touched Carter, and again, the same child's voice we had heard earlier claiming to be the one to have touched Carter said one thing, "David." We missed it the first time. Sometimes in the midst of everything, we don't catch everything said in real time, sometimes we're talking when a voice comes over, and sometimes it takes me playing it over and over in headphones to figure out what is said. But next, I asked specifically what his name was, and again, in the same voice as the two previous responses, he said, "David." My mind was reeling at this point. Several responses by two distinct voices repeatedly was more than I could have ever asked for.

Clayton then asked David if he was hiding behind Carter. No response was given. But in the once chil-

dren's playroom, now set up with display cases so visi-
tors to the museum can learn more about the
Culbertson mansion, was a loud knocking sound from
around one of the exhibits. My heart jumped into my
throat. I quickly looked and turned on my flashlight at
the same time. It was maybe four feet away from me at
the most. It was specifically a light tick and then a loud
thump. Since my focus was so intent on the Odd Box, it
was legit a jump scare.

As the crew and I discussed what we just heard, over
the speaker came loud and clear, "That was us," in an
older female voice. At this point I was covered in goose
bumps, and the hair at the nape of my neck was
standing up. Was it the jump scare, was it a different
voice we hadn't heard before, or did something more
sinister just enter the room?

To calm my nerves, I stayed on target and continued
to ask David questions. I decided that this was the best
course. I didn't want to sever the lines of communication with the child just yet. I then asked David if he was
still by Carter, and almost immediately, it was the small
boy's voice again, this time saying, "I'm in front of him."
And immediately Carter felt electricity on his arm as if
being touched by our new unseen friend. I mean,
WHOA, getting a full sentence on a spirit box is rare,
extremely rare, for anyone, but our first time with the
Odd Box—I couldn't have been happier. Whatever form
of contact we had with this small child at this moment

was unlike anything we had ever experienced before. But it would turn out to be one of the many experiences at this location that has stuck with me over the years.

After this moment, sweet David's voice seemed to fade and became more and more unintelligible. We heard him but couldn't really understand what he was saying anymore. We tried more questions, and he faded out completely.

Again, in the corner just a few feet from me was the knock in the corner, in the same place. I asked in what we call my "mommy voice," which is just what you think it is, the voice your mom would use when she meant business, "Who's in the corner?" A faded child's voice came over with three syllables, but even afterward listening to it repeatedly, we couldn't make out what was said. Clayton then very loudly and firmly asked, "Who is in the corner?" We were all a little on edge at that point. But I was trying to keep calm.

My theory on paranormal investigating is this. These spirits were all humans at one point. Their personality in life will still be their personality in death, and what I tell everyone is, "If someone was an asshole in life, they're going to be an asshole in death." Over the years I have learned to get to know the spirit before making any assumptions. I also have a theory that if someone is an asshole in death, most people think they are a demon, but we'll get into that more later.

I also have another theory. Not all spirits can

communicate in the same way. I don't know if there's a learning curve, or if it's like earning a badge in the Scouts when we are kids. Maybe one ghost can only communicate via EVPs. Maybe some are screams because they must put so much energy into it that on our end it sounds like a scream. Then there are others that sound like a faint whisper, and yet others sound like they are standing in the room with you. There are some spirits that people see walk through walls, yet others can turn a doorknob and open the door. The learning curve is just a theory. OK, back to the investigation.

The loud knock in the corner had us on edge. Was this the spirit trying to communicate, was the spirit trying to scare us, or was it trying to take our focus off the children? After asking who was in the corner, a male voice came over. A gruff, almost elderly voice said, "Me."

I then felt the man's presence, and at the same time, the name "Jackson" came over. When we asked who the man in the corner was, I started feeling a little more about this man. He was a stern man who was not having any shenanigans and was all business. I felt like he was very protective of the home and was maybe a butler or head servant of some sort. Clayton asked why he was here, and immediately the exact same female voice that had said "that was us" came over loud and clear, saying, "Well, you shouldn't be here." I then explained to the spirits that we had permission to be there, that we weren't there to hurt anyone, steal anything, or do anything that would hurt the location. Then I felt a cold breeze come at me directly from the corner. We were on the third floor, no windows were open, and I was nowhere near a door. There was no reason I should feel any breeze, let alone a cold one. As we know, heat rises, and being on the top floor in the summertime, there should have been no cold breezes in the room.

I continued to explain that we were not there for any reason but to document the people in the house like himself. We were not going to hurt the children; we just wanted to tell everyone's story. And as I addressed him again to ask him more questions, as I said his name Jackson, the box said Jackson at the exact same time. But that was the final communication we received from Jackson that night. Out of curiosity, because of the stern vibe the spirit was giving me, I asked Anna if Jackson was who she had been afraid of earlier while we were doing our dowsing rod session, and the response was puzzling at the time. She said, "Mommy, where are you?" But I'd find out in the years to come exactly what it meant.

After no other voices came through, and the feeling of emptiness in the room other than us, we decided to move on to another location in this massive home. We had already spent more time in this one room than we had initially planned on. And we just didn't have the time it would take to get to each room. When we investigate a location, we get the same time allotted as your everyday investigator. We don't have the luxury of a big production crew and several days and nights at a location. So we had to scoot.

We headed back downstairs and discussed what we had just experienced. In all honesty, I myself wasn't expecting much in the way of evidence. Since the place had really never been investigated, it could have gone two ways. I would have sensed spirits within the location, and they wouldn't know how to communicate with us, or what we actually got, which was the Holy Grail of evidence. So, for those who don't know me, I am the most cynical positive person you'll ever meet. One second I'm thinking, *Is this all we'll get on this investigation?* and the next moment I'm thinking, *Holy guacamole, if this is the evidence we got right off the bat, what if they're just warming up? What if they have so much more to tell us? I can't wait to see who else is spending their afterlife here.* But only getting back to investigating would give me the answer I needed.

We headed to the second floor next, which housed the bedrooms for the influential families that lived here over the years. We placed equipment and cameras all over on this floor, but really focused on one of the adult children's rooms of the Culbertson family. It was lavish beyond any of my dreams. The ceilings were the highest I had ever seen, and the walls were painted a lush light sage green. The floor-to-ceiling windows were covered by indoor shutters to keep any outside light or noise at bay. And this room fed into the morning room, where the ladies would spend mornings drinking coffee and catching up with one another, and on the other end it was attached to one of the other adult children's rooms, just as lush, however, painted a pale sky blue, and this one had an antique baby bassinet in it as well. Across the hall was the master bedroom, which was as large as the two bedrooms put together, with a stunning four-poster bed, and every bit as stately as you think it would be, then multiply that by five.

We settled on the green room, and again let any spirits, energies, or entities know we were only there out of light and peace. We again stated that we were not there to hurt them, harm them, or take them away. We let them know that if it helped, they could take some of our energy, and after I say this, I always joke and tell them we drink our energy today, usually taking a sip from my favorite energy drink at the time. I let them know that we'd had communication with some spirits upstairs, hoping to reassure them that it was OK to communicate with us.

Cameras rolling, we got into it, and unbeknownst to any of us, Carter captured what I can only describe as a mist. It wasn't your standard circle dust orb. My feelings on orbs are they are always dust unless they pulsate and give off some sort of energy. Faces spotted in orbs, again, just my opinion, are just people searching for something that isn't there. I personally see faces in everything, from rocks to wooden doors to even sometimes carpeting. It's called pareidolia. It's just not a paranormal phenomenon. But this changed shapes. It was about half an inch wide at its largest point. It billowed and floated right through my head and, coming out the other side, gained brightness and density, yet kept changing shapes. I'm not saying I'm telling you one million percent this was paranormal, but I had just offered up my energy to the spirits that resided there, and then that happened. And as it passed through me, it gained brightness as if gaining some of my energy. My feelings are yes, this was some sort of manifestation that took me up on my offer and took some of my energy.

Clayton decided to run a quick EVP session, and he explained to any entities that might be within earshot how it worked and how we were sometimes able to hear voices on the digital recorder that we might not hear with the naked ear. Clayton proceeded with asking questions while recording, and with my ear during this EVP session, I heard what can only be described as a swoosh next to me, and then I felt electricity all down my right side right afterward. It's said that when people get this feeling of electricity, the best way to describe this feeling is when in the winter, we get that staticky feeling from blankets or many other things when the air is dry, or when you rub a latex balloon on your hair or clothing or anything like that, and your hair just kind of stands up on end without the feeling of goose bumps or coldness. This was the feeling I had all down the right side of my body. My spidey senses were on full alert, and I was pumped.

We played back the recording, where Clayton introduced us by name and asked for anyone to tell us their name. We heard the swoosh I'd heard, which on the recorder sounded more like a loud exhale, and then what sounded like a D or a T at the end of a word in a whisperish tone. If it was a response, it was so faint and so almost distant sounding that we couldn't make out anything that made sense to us. But what it was, and what it meant was there was someone there we could not see who wanted to communicate with us. And that was always a good sign. And it also validated the feeling of electricity I'd felt on my side, as it's said that spirits manifest themselves as energy. Was it the mist we saw? Was it someone we were communicating with upstairs? Only time and more investigating would tell.

Since the electronic voice phenomenon method didn't seem to be working for either us or the entity that was trying to communicate with us, I pulled out a flashlight. When we ask spirits to communicate with us via a flashlight session, we use flashlights that are turned off and on with the flashlight head. Flashlights that are turned off and on with a switch or a button don't work for this. When the head is twisted, it gets the energy from the encased batteries to the light itself. So we set up the flashlight to be barely on. Nine times out of ten this doesn't work. If the flashlight sits in this almost-on stage for too long, sometimes the connection can be made on its own depending on the temperature of the room, the elevation of the location, etc. But when we ask several questions, and they are answered immediately, and the light is turned back off on command, we like to think that it is being manipulated by the unseen entities we are seeking. Not everyone feels this is a form of communication, but with the right circumstances, I truly do.

So the flashlight was set up, and I was explaining to the spirits how to use it when I heard movement in the other bedroom attached to the room we were in. Not footsteps, but the sounds of fabric against fabric, like the sounds a long Victorian dress would make when a lady wearing it would move and walk. Clayton heard it as well, so we went into the room to see if there was a fan or something that would have made the sound, and we found nothing of the sort.

We walked back out of the room to find the flashlight turned on, and it turned off as soon as I noticed it. While this was exciting, it doesn't always denote paranormal activity. All I could do was check to make sure that our static camera in the room was pointing at it, so we could review it later. Upon further review, we noted that this was the only time when we weren't looking that the flashlight turned on and off.

Since this location had never been investigated

before, we continued to encourage the spirits when they did something that we could visually see. And again explained to the entities that none of this equipment or ourselves were here to hurt them. Investigating a place that had never been investigated to this level before is sometimes frustrating, but mostly rewarding. I can't imagine there's a manual that tells the spirits how to communicate with us, and I know damn well we don't have one telling us how to get the communication. It's all trial and error. So we gave it one more try.

As Clayton was speaking with the spirits with the intentions I just listed, I felt my hair move on its own. Let me explain, this is a thing with me. On several occasions at many locations I've felt a slight tug on my hair before paranormal activity gets really good. I've felt this while wearing a hat. I've felt this with my hair tied in a ponytail. Now it's not every single location, but too many for me to keep track of.

But this time it was different. I felt my hair lifted off my shoulder. I have slightly longer than shoulder-length hair, and I felt it levitate for a moment and then fall onto my shoulder again. I checked to make sure there was a camera that could have caught it, and upon review of this footage later, we could see it move, just a few strands lift up and out to the side, and then just drop back down. All of this happened while I was standing completely still, with no major air movement felt by anyone in the room. It wasn't the normal tug or pull I have been known to feel, but it was almost as if something was playing with my hair, like it had stuck its hand up in my hair and then let it go. To be perfectly honest, I'm not even sure how I felt it happen, other than the spirit who was playing with my hair WANTED me to feel it. I was scared at first, but the intentions didn't seem dire or malicious at all, so I let it go and continued to coax the spirits into communicating with us. And just as every other time before when my hair was moved by an unseen force, the activity kicked up tenfold.

Immediately after this I heard loud footsteps in the hallway just outside the room, but not just heavy footsteps, they had a squeak to them, so it was happening in real time. Some footsteps in locations are just residual energy that is left behind. Just something that happened on such a regular basis over many, many years, it's almost like an energetic loop left from the past. But those are always just footsteps. This had a squeak to the floor, and once I walked out in the hallway, I made the same squeak happen with my weight and foot impression. This is not something that I believe residual energy can produce. This is proof that there was something in this hall, a hall we could all see with our peripheral vision, and none of us saw a thing.

Upon entering the room again, I noticed that the flashlight was on again, and I began to feel like the entity was playing with us, distracting us from the flashlight, only to come back in to find it on, or were they learning to use it when we weren't around? And as I entered the room, we all three heard the REM pod go off in what used to be the master bedroom, but unfortunately I forgot to put a static camera on it (again, no production crew, it's just the three of us and loads of equipment), and you know our saying, video or it didn't happen. We went into this room and ran an EVP session in there, and there was no more evidence collected. We left to go back to the room we had been in, but not before putting a camera on the REM pod, and sadly it never went off again in that room.

Clayton then tried an EVP session, only to get no response. Carter then suggested an Odd Box session. Since it worked so well upstairs, it might work at this location as well. It's really hard to say what kind of equipment will get the best response at any location, and this one was no different, so we moved on to the Odd Box. And as earlier, it did not disappoint.

The moment after turning it on, I was trying to explain to the spirits that might be within earshot how it worked, and before I could even finish, as clear as anything, the Odd Box said, "Clayton." To be fair, this is not anything new. Our spirit box has been saying Clayton's name for years. Actually ever since his very first investigation, and we believed that a spirit had attached itself to our spirit box, which was now playing through our Odd Box. In all fairness, it's not every location, but it is more often than not. And it's only through this specific device. And this is what led us to believe this entity, whose name is Walter, is attached to this spirit box.

So picture it if you will, all three of us rolling our eyes, like when that one friend of your shows up and takes your attention away from the exciting time you were having, that's where we were with Walter.

As you can imagine, we were feeling a bit annoyed, as we wanted to talk to the spirits of the house. Clayton asked Walter if he was trying to warn him about something. And in the same voice Clayton's name was said again, followed up by another familiar voice, that of the young girl from upstairs, Anna, saying, "Who's that?" which confirmed our suspicion that the spirit saying Clayton's name on repeat was not from this particular location and had to be Walter.

And this was where Clayton confronted the spirit of Walter, telling him that he'd had enough, that he was sick of the entity just coming over saying his name and not giving any reason. And when Clayton reiterated that he was sick of it, Walter's voice came over and said two words, "Are you?" with an air of sass and confrontation. And then repeated his name twice more in the exact same male voice as had previously come over our Odd Box. This guy's got some ghostly balls.

Moments later, Clayton explained that we were here to communicate with the spirits of the house and that he wanted him to leave, and in the same voice again, Walter came through loud and clear, saying two different phrases, "Not yet," and a beat later, "Won't leave." And yes, we should be happy about this very direct, very clear communication with the other side, but again, we weren't here to talk to a spirit that's been interrupting our investigations for what's been seven years now.

As Clayton was having it out with Walter, which he should have done a long time ago, I felt a hand on my shoulder as if to say, *hey, we're still here*, coming from the spirits that actually resided at this location. That was when we switched gears and ignored Walter and directed our questions to the spirits of the house itself. We asked several questions to the spirits of the location, and Clayton's name was still being said. I then asked any spirits that might be there with us, "Do you know Anna and David from upstairs?" and over a ridiculous amount of sweeps in a row came Walter's voice, saying, "This is… Walter… not really."

And we decided that it was time to let the Odd Box rest in this room of the house. I honestly in my heart of hearts felt as though the other spirits wanted to communicate with us, but Walter was not letting them. We were frustrated and decided to move on. But not before I was hit with an overwhelming sense of dizziness, so much so that I felt like I might pass out. Was this the repercussions of the misty anomaly taking energy from me when we first stepped in the room? My gut told me yes, and I felt the need to take a step outside to clear my head.

After several moments, I started feeling better and decided to continue finding out the story of this amazing mansion.

For this next investigation, Clayton and I decided to split up. He had his heart set on investigating the child's weird time-out closet up on the top floor of the servants' quarters, and I was dying to investigate the dining room. It was gorgeous, and a woman in a green dress had been spotted there on more than one occasion.

Clayton headed upstairs with a flashlight, an infrared video camera, an EVP recorder, and a walkie-talkie so that we could still communicate if need be. Carter and I headed to the dining room with the Odd Box, a spirit box, a few cameras and the dowsing rods. We rarely separate like this, but with a location as sprawling as this one, there's no way we would be able to cover as much as we wanted to in the brief amount of time we had there if we didn't spread out a bit.

With Clayton on the third floor in this odd little time-out closet, which was an average-size closet, but made completely out of lattice so that you could completely see through it, at the very top of the servants' stairway, and me and Carter on the first floor, we began setting up, and used the walkie-talkies to make sure any sounds we heard weren't each other.

As Carter went to close the door in the dining room, hoping to block out any noise contamination, Clayton radioed us from the time-out closet, trying to conduct a flashlight session without much success. He asked if we were moving furniture, and I let him know that Carter was closing doors, so that Clayton didn't mistake any noise traveling up the stairs as paranormal activity. He'd then mark it on his camera recording verbally.

As soon as I was done telling him my plan to conduct an Odd Box session in the dining room, Clayton's flashlight, which had been at a static off position for nearly ten minutes straight, was now pulsing on and off gently. Clayton then asked the energy to turn it all the way on so that he knew it wasn't just a coincidence. He waited as it continued to just pulsate a very low light. He was startled by the fact that I came over the walkie-talkie again, asking if he heard the REM pod going off, and as soon as my voice came across, the flashlight went to full on instantly.

I ran upstairs as quickly as I could to check on the REM pod, but by the time I had gotten up there, I could no longer hear it going off. And even after checking the GoPro that sat filming the REM pod, it never did go off. So I'm not sure to this day what that could have been.

We were now about to settle in for our separate investigations. Clayton continued to coax the flashlight into turning on again, to no avail. And I finally got settled in to begin my and Carter's investigation in the formal dining room. Clayton began to feel frustrated at the lack of responses on the third floor, and he radioed down to me and Carter, telling us he was only having luck with the flashlight when we were communicating via the walkie-talkie. And in true smart-ass fashion, I responded, "Well, send them my way." And not even a full second after I said this, the flashlight turned on full blast as bright as it possibly could. And this confirmed Clayton's thought, that it was my voice that was getting the response from the flashlight. Which was so odd, because Clayton was the one who usually gets all the responses from the flashlight sessions. And I then asked if it was Anna, the spirit whom I couldn't seem to stop thinking about the entire night, and the flashlight just stayed fully lit.

As I tried to figure out what this phenomenon could be, I continued to run my investigation of the dining room, and to tell you the truth, I am known to suck up to the spirits to try to get a response. I said out loud, "This is a lovely dining room. Can I speak to the lady of the house?" I got no responses. I asked for them to please tell us their story. All the while, Clayton was upstairs, trying to ask the spirit who was interacting with the earlier questions, trying to figure out who it is. The flashlight continued to stay off the entire time. He asked if it was a child, he asked if it was an adult, and absolutely nothing happened. And I was still getting no responses in the dining room as well.

Since he was getting no real response, he radioed Carter and me down in the dining room just to check in.

I responded, asking what he had just said, because I was not even paying attention. I was trying so hard to get evidence in the dining room.

When Clayton heard my response, he was watching the flashlight, which had been sitting turned off for so long. And sure as anything, the flashlight turned on full power again.

I mean, how was this even possible?

We discussed my coming up, to see if I could get a response from the spirit, and we could finally figure out what was going on, but we decided to stay separate, and I would just radio my questions from the first floor, since it was working already. And as my dad always said: If it's not broke, don't fix it.

I settled in, got comfy, and tried out this new paranormal investigation technique we just happened to literally stumble on.

Clayton placed the walkie-talkie up close to the flashlight, and we began. My first question was directly to Anna. I asked her, "Are you there with my friend Clayton?" And yep, you guessed it, the flashlight turned on full brightness. Clayton let me know that the flashlight turned on. With my mind blown, I told Clayton, "This is absolutely insane," and I told Anna, "We really appreciate you communicating with us." This energy, or spirit, was helping us understand how best to communicate with her. We'd met her on the third floor just maybe fifty yards from where Clayton was now. Maybe she wasn't able to leave that floor, but still wanted to communicate with me. I was elated and nervous at the same time. But the way I investigate is, I just go with the flow, in this case the flow that this spirit was giving me.

I then said over the walkie-talkie, "Anna, someone told me about you before I came here. I believe I was sent here to help you. Do you need help?" To that question I got no response. Which was actually a good thing. When I am investigating and a spirit asks us to help them, I am always sad, as I don't know how to help them. I know how to communicate with them, I know how to tell their story via filming and editing a video, but to actually physically help them, I am always at a loss.

Since it was clear she didn't need help, I then asked her, "Do you like staying here, Anna?" To which Clayton informed me, with a chuckle in his voice, "Holy shit, it just turned full on."

All of our minds were reeling at this point, and we were amazed at the response we were getting with a method the spirit of Anna had just taught us. Clayton then suggested bringing the Odd Box back up to the third floor with Carter and me so that we could have a real-time conversation with her. As Carter and I packed up and made our way up the servants' staircase, Clayton explained to the unseen spirit, who had just all but proven she was there, exactly what we were going to do next. And then Clayton asked the spirit we now knew was Anna if she would communicate with him. The flashlight remained on from the last question I had asked and gotten a response to. He then asked Anna, "Can you turn off the flashlight if you'd rather talk to Kitsie?" Then the flashlight turned completely off.

Clayton radioed to tell us what was happening up in the time-out closet, which he had not left the entire time. I radioed up to Clayton on my way up that I heard the REM pod again on the second floor, so I was going to stop and check the batteries. And the moment I started talking, the flashlight on the floor next to Clayton went instantly to full on.

This was the first time we had ever had any spiritual communication via walkie-talkie before, and to my knowledge, it's the first time a spirit only demanded to talk to one of us in particular. Sometimes in the past, some of us will have more luck at a location than others. Sometimes spirits prefer one of us to the other, but never would ONLY communicate with just one of us. This was the first time where a spirit would only reach out if it heard one particular voice.

I could not wait to find out more about this spirit who called herself Anna. I wanted to know why she chose me. I was positive she had a story to tell, and was honored that she chose me. My mind was reeling. Had this ever happened to any other investigator? I know for a fact it had never happened to me or my team. As I reach the Rem pod, it was silent. And I wondered to myself, *Was this another spirit beckoning me upstairs, or was it Anna?*

I headed up the next flight of stairs with the Odd Box, the walkie-talkie, my flashlight, and camera in hand. As I reached the top of the stairs, I had the urge to instantly start talking to Anna. I let her know I was there, and asked her if she could hear me, and I asked her to turn the flashlight on for yes. As I was saying this, I was thinking in my head, *What if this doesn't work? What if she prefers to keep communicating like we were?* As I was thinking this, I felt an unseen entity touch me, and at the same time, I heard Clayton gasp, still in the time-out closet. And I heard him exclaim, "It's fucking on." I think at that moment, we were all relieved that the lines of communication were still open. But who had touched my shoulder? Was it Anna saying hello? Did she gently touch me walking past to turn the flashlight on? In my heart of hearts I knew this was the case. I was so excited to see what would happen next.

I hurriedly worked on getting the Odd Box all set up so we could have more real-time communication, and so I could ask more than yes and no questions. When I was nearly finished setting up, I asked her if she was ready to use the Odd Box like we had before. And we got no response. We waited; still no response. I reached down to turn it on, and Carter said, "Wait. She hasn't turned the light on yet. Wait until she says it's OK." So I told her this was what I had been using when she communicated with us earlier, and I reminded her that it wouldn't hurt her. Still no response. I was terrified we'd lost her, that she'd maybe run out of energy and was unable to communicate with us any longer. My shoulders dropped. When this happens, it's not only disappointing, but it's sad. It's like meeting a new person who you really like right off the bat and want to know all about them, and in the middle of them telling you about themselves, they just up and disappear.

I then asked Anna if she was in the hallway with me instead of in the closet with Clayton.

After a good ten to fifteen seconds, the flashlight turned on fully. It was delayed, though, and not as instantaneous as it had been. So we weren't sure what that would mean, other than she was in the hallway with me and went back in to the tiny room to turn the flashlight on. It was exciting and confusing at the same time.

But when I went to continue with my questioning, I heard what could have been a female voice, but could have been Carter burping right behind me. Whenever I hear something that could pass as any type of gas, that's usually my go-to. Nine times out of ten, weird noises are one of our stomachs. I asked Carter if he had just burped, because I didn't want to assume that I was hearing a spirit at the time, because we hadn't heard anything like that the entire evening. But Carter's response was negative. And I knew then it was a female voice I had heard. I had no idea what it had said until the evidence was reviewed. Clayton asked if it was a young female voice, and I responded yes, and that it came from the nanny's room, which was right behind me up a few stairs, with the door open.

Upon evidence review, we discovered that it was a young female's voice that said the name "Christina." And this is ridiculously amazing, because my name is Christina. Kitsie is a nickname I've had since I was a little girl. I absolutely always introduce myself to the spirits as Kitsie. However, whenever Clayton gets really excited about evidence, or is scared and needs to get my attention, and, I will say, every time he radioed me to let me know about the flashlight turning on, he called me Christina. So this spirit we were assuming was Anna was either really paying attention, or she was able to tell more about me than any information I had given her.

The EVP we captured was on the camera Carter was holding at the time. It sounded 100% female, and the age was certainly not a young child, but could have been a young adult or woman in a breathy slight whisper. It was bone chilling the first time I heard it; however, it didn't sound threatening in any way. But the fact that it was audible to our ears clearly says to me she wanted to be heard.

I then hooked up the Odd Box and set the settings perfectly. And I told Anna I would love to hear her pretty voice again, and asked Anna to tell us hello. And immediately we heard the same voice we had heard earlier in the evening telling us her name was Anna. And what she said was, "Hello," the moment after I had asked her to. I heard Clayton exclaim, still in the time-out closet, "WHAT?!" All of our minds were blown. Remember, we weren't expecting any evidence in the location to begin with, and somehow, we'd made a solid connection with one specific entity. This was unprecedented for us up until this point. But I was ready to hear this girl's story, so I pressed on.

Clayton let me know that the flashlight had finally turned off. So I asked the teenage spirit that I seem to have bonded with if she'd come out into the hallway and speak to me. Where Carter and I were standing, the servants' stairway landing on the third floor, was just outside what had been the nanny's room back in the heyday of the home. And just moments later, the Odd Box belted out, "I wanna," and after another second, it said, "I do."

I then asked her a few more questions with no response on the Odd Box. I wondered if she'd left or had run out of energy, and asked her if she was still with us. She responded with, "I'm here," and I then asked her to turn on the flashlight that she had been communicating with us on earlier, which was located on the floor next to Clayton, who was still in the punishment closet. And the light turned on immediately.

After turning off the Odd Box, I moved closer to the closet, which was again not your normal closet. There are several diamond-shaped holes in it, so anyone outside can see in easily, especially in a dark hallway like the one we were currently in. I then asked out loud, as I had been, and sitting down right outside the tiny little room, "Is it OK if I sit here near you?" And we all with bated breath watched the flashlight turn immediately off, as if she was telling us yes. I could only assume either this was her preferred form of communication, or this was the easiest for her.

Ready to find out more about this young lady, I asked her if her last name was Culbertson, and we got no response. I then asked her if her last name was McDonald, to which we also got no response.

I then shifted my line of questioning, and I asked, "Did you go to school close to here?" And she immediately turned the flashlight on. But that was the last flashlight response we got for that little Q&A session with all of us either in or huddled around the time-out room. Question after question went unanswered by the flashlight.

Not ready to give up on Anna yet, I felt like she had left me, and I wanted so much more. I pulled out my walkie-talkie while sitting right there, and asked if she'd like to go back to talking this way. The flashlight did nothing. But as soon as I pressed the button down and said, "Anna, are you still here?" the flashlight turned on immediately again.

As I got up, Carter asked if they could hear our

voices better through the walkie-talkies. And it could really be a thing, and there's no way to prove it. I blurted out, "Maybe it's like their spirit box." And we all got goose bumps.

I then walked down the hallway and up the three stairs into the nanny's room, to avoid feedback on the walkie-talkies. The nanny's room was very simple, a large room with a bed, a chest of drawers, and an armoire.

Once in the nanny's room, Carter's camera caught a light anomaly above my head, pulsating as it floated like it had its very own light source. It was round and about the average size of your standard dust orb. You know the ones most people think are ghosts? But are one million percent just dust that statically reflects the infrared light coming off the cameras. But this wasn't a static light. It flashed on and off. And this had only happened once before and floated over my head in the same way. And has never happened again.

I began the questions again. I asked her If I could talk to her through here, and the light instantly turned on. Clayton let us know since we could no longer see what was going on in the closet he remained in.

I continued with my questioning. I asked her into the walkie-talkie, "Can you come into the nanny's room with me?" and after a few seconds, the flashlight just barely turned on, almost as if she was hesitant. If you recall, she had been afraid of the nanny earlier. Since I sensed a hesitation, I let her know she could stay where she was if she wanted to, and the flashlight instantly went to full on, as if to say thank you.

Just after that, I heard a baby crying off in the distance. I asked the boys if they heard the same thing, and neither of them did. But I know what I heard. They laughed it off, but I reiterate that I legit heard a baby crying. And this was when stuff started to get really weird for me, and for the crew as well. Clayton felt a breeze go by him, and then the flashlight turned on without any questions being asked. All I had said before this was I heard a baby crying.

I then told Clayton I had felt a breeze not ten seconds before he said that, and where the breeze came from was in the hallway, just seconds before I heard the baby, the same hallway where Clayton had seen the shadow figure on the ceiling earlier in the evening. And this was where the plot thickened.

I heard the crying baby again, the cry of a newborn baby. Again I was the only one who heard it. I told the boys what I was hearing, and the flashlight turned full off immediately. Neither of them heard the baby this time either, but the fact that the flashlight reacted both times had Carter saying out loud, "You might be hearing something, then." Which was ridiculously validating to me and made me a feel a little less crazy. I love it when the evidence backs me up.

After a beat I asked, "Anna, is there a baby here with

us?" To which the flashlight gave no response. Clayton then asked me to ask her, "Is the baby I hear crying yours, Anna?" And the flashlight immediately went to completely on after I asked her the question through the radio. I mean, WHOA! Just you wait, it gets even better, I promise.

We were all BLOWN AWAY at this point, and I say at the very least.

I gasped and said to the boys, and not through the radio, "Maybe she doesn't have a baby anymore." Right after I said this, Carter said that something just touched his arm. And Clayton exclaimed from the closet that he was suddenly covered in goose bumps. And the light next to him remained fully on.

I then clicked the button on my walkie-talkie and asked, "Anna, did you lose a baby?" And the flashlight turned completely off.

Our moods completely changed, and we all had a heavy feeling of sadness, and I let Anna know into the radio just how sorry we were for her loss.

And this was where I had a moment, a moment where I saw a memory that's not mine. Which I have been told by renowned medium Tiffany Rice is the spirit showing me their memory. I saw a small room, not elaborate in any way, I assume it's in the servants' quarters, with a few servants around a table. On the table is a very young woman with no wedding ring, giving birth and having a really hard time of it, with a man in very regal clothing anxiously awaiting nearby. I see the servants in a panic, like something has gone horribly wrong. It was a horrible sight to see. And I somehow just knew the mother was Anna. A fifteen-year-old giving birth in the nineteenth century wasn't unheard of, but I knew now that Anna was a servant girl. But who was the father? Was it another servant? He certainly wasn't dressed like one. Or was it one of the sons of the head of the house, or even worse, the man of the house at the time?

I asked Anna again, through the walkie-talkie, "Were there complications during your childbirth?" wondering if this was how she died, or the baby died, or both. The flashlight stayed steadily off. I then asked, "Do you not want to talk about the baby?" And the flashlight flickered briefly and went to full on. I then let her know, "It's OK. We don't have to talk about it."

At this point, it was already pushing past the wee hours of the morning, and with the mood shift, I was struggling with what questions to ask. And we decided to try with a last-ditch effort to see if maybe Anna could talk through the walkie-talkies. Our thoughts were if she could hear us better through this device, maybe if Clayton held down the button in the place where she was responding, maybe, just maybe, we'd get some sort of response.

The moment Clayton picked up the walkie-talkie, the light flickered from full off to full on and back to full off, after being steadily off for quite some time. Clayton then continued to explain to Anna what we were trying to do, and that he would hold the button down , and he asked her to talk directly to me through it. As Clayton explained everything that was going to happen, I was sure to set up a digital recorder right in front of my walkie-talkie. And deep down I was skeptical about this. And I hoped I wasn't setting my team up for disappointment. But when Clayton pressed the button down, we waited, not long, but we waited, and instead of what was once just the sound of dead air, I heard static come over my radio. Bursts of static that, to me, were in a cadence of someone speaking. And I told the boys out loud, "I feel like she's trying."

And Carter responded, "There's something trying to come through."

And then the static stopped. Clayton still had his finger on the button, so now it was just dead air again. I then asked her, "Can you try a little harder to come through? Feel free to take energy from any of us." And immediately the static started up again. It was spotty, again like she was trying. We have no definitive proof that this is documented spirit communication, but it was something, and all of us there that night know, in our heart of hearts, this was real, she was trying, and she was communicating. But sadly we could not make out what she was saying. And every time I would ask Anna a question, it would do the same thing. If I was talking to the boys, it wouldn't do anything. At one point, I had asked her if she was turning sixteen on her next birthday, and the response to that question was one short burst of static, which would have been the perfect amount of time to say either yes or no. And nothing else came over until I asked the next question. And the next question was answered with several bursts of static as if it was a full sentence.

As you can imagine, our minds were blown. But our batteries were running low on most of our equipment, so we knew we had to come to a close. I knew that Anna was afraid up there, and I asked her to come downstairs with us, and as I was talking, the light turned on for the first time in a long while. So we grabbed our things, brought everything downstairs, and packed up the equipment and cameras and headed back home.

Usually after every investigation, we smudge ourselves. Smudging is the burning of a dried bundle of sage, and you set your intentions while burning it. We surround each other in the smoke of the sage and set our intentions that no energies or entities are allowed to follow us home, that we are surrounded by love, light, peace, and positivity, and we thank the spirits for their time. And we go on our merry way and review the footage later. Chris drove Carter and me home, and Carter drove to his house, and Clayton drove back to his place.

And we thought all was done, that we had gathered

amazing evidence, and that we did what we always hope to do, tell the story of those at the location who want us to tell it.

But then, about a week later, I noticed my one-year-old Neapolitan mastiff playing with something that wasn't there. And I didn't think much of it. Until it kept happening over and over again. Until one day, it struck me that this might be Anna. So out loud I said, sitting in my living room, with just me and the dogs, "Anna, if that's you, can you bring Tasha to me?" And lo and behold, my super-stubborn mastiff came walking straight over to me. If I had asked her to come to me, there's no way it would have happened. And I tried it again, mind you, I was never able to teach this dog any commands other than sit. She was special, may she rest in peace. I asked Anna to make her walk in a circle, and lo and behold, the sweet, but not so bright, 150-pound, full of wrinkles and sagging jowls mastiff walked in a perfect circle around nothing at all. That was the day I realized I had brought Anna home with me, and she's still here to this day. She has come with me on investigations, and I know this because her voice comes over. She even once came across on someone else's ITC device called a hack shack. That particular device was in Australia. Every once and a while I will hear footsteps in my bedroom upstairs while downstairs in the living room, and I just smile.

We cohabitate nicely. I have rules, and she adheres to

them. I think, yes, I pretty much accidentally told her she could follow me. But being in a place like that, with the horrible memories she had there, I understand why she's here, so I don't ask her to leave, and I don't expect her to any time soon.

CHAPTER 2

VARIOUS LOCATIONS

I learn so much on each investigation.

I have been to so many locations over the years, and each place has taught me something. Right now I'm going to cover several locations and tell you short snippets from each location that stuck with me. If I were to do a deep dive into each part of each location, we'd both be here way longer than we'd care to.

* * *

Old Lake County Jail and Sherriff's House. Crown Point, Indiana

THIS IS the location I have been to the most over the years, and I still want to go back many, many more times. It's close to my heart because it's in the county I grew up in. And I never knew what this place was until I was looking for places to investigate in my home state, and I jumped at the chance to investigate there. I arrived with my husband and a couple of friends. I had no idea what to expect. I had never investigated a jail before, and going in, I had no idea how sinister a jail could be. But I found out very quickly.

We set up for the evening with infrared cameras and the little bit of equipment I had at the time. This was only the fifth place I had investigated. The first being a very old Victorian home, the second being an old elementary school, and the third being Ferry Plantation, where I saw my very first apparition, and the fourth place was an old gymnasium in Southern Indiana, with the same people who were here with me today, Chris, my husband, and Tony and Jenny, whom we had been friends with for years.

We took the tour, and we were all pretty jovial, until we weren't. Our first place to investigate was a cellblock. It seriously looks like it's straight out of a horror movie. This specific cellblock is the exact same one that John Dillinger escaped from back in the day the Mob ran Chicago. Lake County, Indiana, which is also known as Northwest Indiana, is just a hop, skip, and a jump from Chicago, so many of the big guys we've all heard about would have safe houses in this area, and all of Northern Indiana, actually.

We started out at the very end of the cellblock, which

was known as the dayroom, where convicts would hang out during the day when they weren't in their cells. This room was pretty much just a larger cell with a picnic-style table set up for socializing. At this point the table was there and that was about it.

We settled in and started a question and answer session with a K2 meter. This device is said to pick up electromagnetic fields, and it's said that spirits can put off levels of electricity themselves. And at the time it was my most important device. We had set one up on the bars that separate the room from the hallway, facing into the cell or the room, and I began asking questions. We heard some slight tapping coming from the other end of the cellblock; then my husband, Chris, said he felt as though something was passing close to him on several occasions. It's hard to explain this feeling if you've never felt it before, but the best way to describe it is, you know when you're looking down, or not looking at the door to a room, and you can just FEEL someone coming in without hearing or seeing them. Well, that's exactly what it feels like. Then our Ovilus said the word "loving," and I distinctly remember my husband saying that was the last word he had thought he'd hear in a prison. And we were still hearing that slight tapping noise coming from the other end of the cellblock.

Sandy, the head of Paranormal Investigations and one hell of a historian, had told us about the spirit that is said to hang out in this cellblock. This inmate was James

"Fur" Sammons. This man was the worst of the worst and went by the nickname Fur. He was called this because of his preference for the lack of bikini-area grooming, which is the nicest way I can say it. This man was arrested the first time at the age of sixteen for being a party in the gang rape of an eleven-year-old girl. He and four others beat her, raped her, and tried to strangle her. He was the worst of the worst. And he was a career criminal the rest of his life. But he was finally caught in Cedar Lake, Indiana, and placed in Crown Point Jail. On November 31, 1933, he was found guilty in an Indiana court of bribing an official and being a habitual criminal, and sentenced for life.

He had killed many in his lifetime and was considered a psychopath. And he was known in mob circles as Capone's Mad Man. And of course, this was the entity that had decided to communicate.

I had honestly not been scared in my other investigations. On edge, yes, as this was still so new to me, and some locations I had felt more comfortable in than others. But this jail was HUGE, and so many bad people had been in and out of it over the years, so many bad things can only have happened there as well. And then this guy decided to come and play the proverbial ball with us, I was on edge to say the least, but at this point in my career, so many people had told me never to show fear, so what did I do? I flirted with the man who seemed to love the ladies so much. I told him I was dying to meet him and that he should come on down to say hello.

The cellblock is known for shadow figures and black masses, so I, with my inexperience, started to try to harass him just little bit. I said, "Fur, if that's you, for being such a big, strong, and scary man, those taps are awful dainty coming from down the hallway." Still no activity from the K2 until my friend Tony stepped out of the doorway into the dayroom. I started to see light play just outside the cell where the K2 meter was. I got up and stepped into the doorway where my six-foot-five-inch friend had just been standing, and as I did, the K2 meter went off. I mean, it was completely understandable the spirit didn't want to get close to Tony. He was also an ex-prison guard.

So now that the K2 was going off, it was time to ask the questions, to see just who this could be. I stepped out of the doorway, because, well, nerves, and I asked if it was a guard, to no response. We asked if it was a deputy, nothing. We asked if it was the sheriff, and nothing again. So I headed back up to the doorway where I had been standing when it originally went off, and again nothing. We were stumped. So I tried flirting again, and I let them know that I wore my booty jeans just for the prisoners. And nothing. I was slightly offended.

Moments later, the Ovilus said two words. First, "reason," and as we were trying to figure out what that could mean in relation to what we were going through at that exact moment, it said another word, "solo." And this was where I started to freak out a lot, and also started to regret my choice of flirting with this spirit. We were just questioning why the K2 activity had stopped, and the Ovilus told us there was a reason, and the reason was that it would like me solo out in the hallway with no one else. Yep, I was instantly terrified, my heart was racing, and I was starting to sweat in the early spring temps of the low 40 degrees of the location. I was cracking jokes with the crew, playing it off like I wasn't scared, but I did not want to go out in that hallway alone. Something was telling me not to do it.

Looking back, I'm not sure what I was afraid of; there are never headlines that say "Murder Victim Killed by Ghost." Logic tells us that these spirits can't hurt us, but at that moment in time, every horror movie I had ever seen was flashing through my head; then Tony offered to go out in the hallway. And that was when I decided to put on my big-girl panties and just do it. Several deep breaths later, I walked out into the hallway, and I told whoever this spirit was, in my gut I knew it was Fur, that they had until the count of ten and I was going back in. The countdown began. I started with ten, nine and got to seven, and I heard loud footsteps out in the hallway, and I screamed, "Holy shit," and ran back into the cell. As I got back in there, the K2 meter went off, and the digital recorder Chris was listening to with headphones went to complete static.

I was just about to sit back down and hang out with the crew when the Ovilus and its electronic "mouth" said, "Return," as if it wanted me back out in that hallway that seemed so scary to me. I mean, at that point, it was a triple dog dare, and I couldn't say no. As I walked out, I said down the hallway, "You are not allowed to touch me," and stood outside the dayroom, waiting for whatever the spirit had in store for me. I timidly walked out into the hallway all by myself again. Mind you, in the dark I could still see everyone, they were just behind the bars, but at this point in my career, it was so scary.

I was in the hallway, and I asked the energy to light up the K2 meter again, and nothing happened. But against my better judgment, I decided to stay out there a little longer, hoping this would be what it took to communicate with the other side. I started to hear movement to my right; the area to my right was the hallway that connected cellblocks C and D and also led to the stairs that can get you through the entire prison. As I mentioned this to the crew, the K2 meter went off again. Then I mentioned that I was covered in goose bumps from head to toe, and the K2 meter went off again. I said to any entity who might be there, "Hey, how ya doin'?" And then I heard as though a man whispered in my ear, "Hello." I swear I felt the heat of his breath as well. And that was it for that trip to the hallway, I noped my way right out of there and joined the rest of the crew.

They asked me what it was that I was afraid of, and I honestly had no response that would make any sense, other than flight over fight won in this case. Again, looking back, this was a pivotal investigation for me. It taught me that spirits really can't hurt you. I broke through a level of fear I had been fighting since as long as I can remember. Then I headed back out with much less whining this time, the K2 meter in my hand. No sooner had I exited when , the K2 sensed spirit activity.

My hands were shaking, but I was determined to get answers so I began to ask questions. Suddenly,I was interrupted by the loud metallic squeak of a door swinging open and closed. I wasn't the only person who heard this, EVERYONE heard this time. . At this point everyone was a little freaked out. I have to admit I was feeling better that I wasn't the only one who heard the sound, you could say I felt vindicated. I went back into the dayroom and cowered close to the corner of the room while we all asked several questions. No responses came at all.

Chris mentioned that the activity had come to a complete halt and that he thought it was interested in me. To prove his assumption he asked me to step back toward the K2 meter.

I did as he asked, but I'll say that I was nervous even

to take these few steps. When I drew close to the K2 meter it sounded for a solid ten seconds. Immediately, Chris also heard static on the live digital recorder again. . I was startled but wasn't deterred. I then asked, "Is this where you want me to stand?"

The K2 meter lit up for ten seconds. .

The next question asked was, "Does she remind you of your wife or girlfriend?" And the K2 meter lit up just like the last two times. And then suddenly I felt at ease. I didn't know why, maybe it was because we finally were getting to the bottom of why this spirit was singling me out, or maybe that gave me a sense of relief that they liked me and didn't want to hurt me. Again just like being terrified, I couldn't explain really why I wasn't anymore. I responded to this question with a very warmhearted, "Hi."

Tony then told the spirit he was a lucky man. The K2 lit up again fully for several seconds. Then he asked, "Is it a long time since you've seen her?" and the K2 meter showed the same response. Tony then asked if he was alone, and we got no response. Then out of the blue the Ovilus said, "Harriett," and I asked if his wife's name was Harriett; no response. I asked if I reminded him of Harriett, and the K2 meter lit up again.

We still didn't know definitively who this was, but in my heart, I knew it was Fur. And I went from being in full terror mode into "awwww, this isn't so bad." Until I felt what I would have to describe as a hand on my ass.

Yep, you guessed it, I was nowhere where anyone there could have touched me, and just to give you a little more proof that it wasn't any of the crew, I was standing in a corner with a wall on one side and the prison bars on the other. I asked the spirit we had been chatting with if it was him, to no response, so I asked a question that he had answered affirmatively, and no response. I asked if he was still there, and again no response. Then the Ovilus chimed in again and said, "Deplete." Apparently this was our visitor telling us they had no more energy to communicate; it had depleted. And that was when it ended. No more communication that night in the dayroom. But I wanted to know so much more. Why was this murderer, rapist and so much more being nice to me? Who was Harriet? Fur never married; maybe it was a longtime girlfriend, or even his sister or mother.

The next time I returned to the Old Lake County Jail was probably three years later. We had added to our crew a little, but that was the perfect place to have a large crew. We investigated more places than we did the last time, but I ended on an investigation of one of the cells in the C block. I wanted to know if Fur remembered me. I was more confident in my investigative style at this point, and I was ready to find out more about him. So I took Clayton with me, and a cigarette to bribe him with. And after being scared to near death by a bat we didn't expect to see flying right at us, I headed to the cell furthest down from where I had investigated last.

The cell was so tiny, two beds stacked on top of each other, and maybe a four-foot passage to the back of the cell where the latrine was. I walked in and leaned against the bunks. And I said, "Fur, are you here? Do you remember me?" And the silence was deafening. We weren't using any equipment at the time. We just wanted to play it old school. In all honesty, I wanted to hear his voice again, like I had in my ear three years earlier. I then asked again, "Fur, are you here?" and I told him, "I brought a cigarette for you if you cooperate." And I heard a noise in the cell with me. So I pulled out the K2 meter, the same one I had used years before, and I asked him to light it up if it was him. It did just like it did years before.

I then turned on the spirit box that scans very quickly through radio stations, but it's said that any direct response to a question you may have just asked, or anything relative to your investigation, is a paranormal response. And the first word that came over was "Kitsie." Um, OK, Fur, you've got my attention. I asked what I could do for him, and the spirit box, plain as day, said, "Kiss." I let him know that I hardly knew him and that I didn't kiss a man on the first date. I then asked him who Harriet was to him, and the spirit box said, "Love."

My mind was blown. It was like the investigation three years ago had just picked up where we left off. And then nothing.

One theory I've come up with is spirits require a lot of energy to communicate. And when a place is investigated weekend after weekend, I feel like the spirits don't always have the energy to continue with communication. The first time we had investigated this location was in early spring, right after the location had come off its winter break. This time it was late summer, and the place had been investigated A LOT that year before we had gotten in to do our investigation. Maybe that had something to do with it. Maybe the fact that I had brought Harriet up again had him feeling sad. We tried a flashlight session, and the K2 meter again, and nothing. To say I was disappointed would be an understatement.

We decided to call it quits after no responses over a span of about fifteen to twenty minutes, and as I was about to leave, I said out loud, "Hey, Fur, we're leaving. How about a goodbye kiss?" And, kids, be careful what you wish for. I turned to leave the cigarette for him on the top bunk, turned back around to face the wall, and that was the moment I got my first and hopefully only ghost kiss. I felt, on my lips, what I would have to describe as the feeling of butterfly wings on my mouth. I know, no one believes me, but it's true. I have never felt it since, but I've also not asked again for a kiss from a spirit. When I think about it, it's like I feel it all over again. So weird, and so unprovable, but I pinky promise, this is exactly what happened. Yep, I freaked out, and yeah, I totally wiped my had over my lips. Not sure if I offended him or not, but I've been back to that jail one other time, and Fur did not come out to play that night. I hope this isn't the end of his story. But I'll keep you posted.

Harrodsburg Herald

So my theory, like I said, is if someone is an asshole in life, they are going to be an asshole in death. There are not demons at every location, and there are a lot of assholes that I've met in my lifetime, but never a demon. Why would we expect every spirit to come across to be sweet and excited for us to come in and bother them, in the dead of night, at what has become their place to live?

I mean, if someone showed up to my house at 3 a.m. and was provoking me and demanding I answer their questions, or talk into a recorder, or touch some piece of equipment, I would get pissed, I'd tell them to get out, I'd even throw a punch or scratch them. Do you see what I'm getting at? My grandpa always had a saying, you catch more flies with honey, and he's right. Do you think if you're rude to anyone, they wouldn't want to do what these ghosts do that are assumed to be demons? I mean, I used to waitress for a bit, and yeah, I wanted to punch quite a few people. But I didn't, I got nicer and tried to let them know I was there to help them, and you know what? A lot of the times they would come around, and some of those specific people were some of the best tippers. What I'm saying is when I investigate, I try to work at the spirit's comfort level, but sometimes you get the one guy, the guy you have to give back what he's dishing out. You have to get on their level before they'll cooperate with you, but this is very rare.

The Harrodsburg Herald was one of these locations. It's located in Harrodsburg, Kentucky, not that far from the Bourbon Trail. It's a gorgeous quaint little town, and near the center of town is the town newspaper building. The Harrodsburg Herald is on Kentucky's oldest street and was built in the 1800s. It's still running and operating today. There are several spirits in this location, and on this trip, I felt we met many. But this location boasts some pretty big claims. It's said to have a spirit in the warehouse that has thrown an investigator across the room, and other violent attacks. But this spirit specifically hated women. There were several occasions where female investigators were called awful names. In EVPs, the most often captured are "slut" and "bitch."

We started off the evening's investigation in the warehouse specifically. And it's a warehouse. There are shelves upon shelves of office supplies and paper products, loads of boxes and quite a few copy machines and a couple of drawing desks. It's large with maybe ten-foot ceilings, and I couldn't wait to see if the location lived up to the hype. Carter, Clayton and I set up the equipment. We brought with us a REM pod, an EVP recorder, and a spirit box hooked up to the Odd Box, and we were ready to roll.

I went in with my guard slightly up, but not much. I didn't get any bad vibes in the warehouse at all. But we started the investigation as we always do. Even though this location had been investigated many, many times, we set up that level of respect from the beginning, we explained how the equipment worked, we let them know we were there out of love, light, peace, and positivity, and we asked they treat us the same. And I added specifically for any location where it's said to have malevolent activity, if you're rude or harmful to us, we will give it back in return.

I had Clayton start off with a quick EVP session, to which we got no response. We tried to get a response. And we joked around that the REM pod was broken. We have never gotten a definitive response with this piece of equipment, so it's kind of become a running joke every time we ask a spirit to use it.

At this point, I personally was getting bored, not a single response from the big bad spirit that was said to be there, or any of the others. So to break the monotony, I hooked up the spirit box to the Odd Box, and it immediately said, "Good morning." Which was odd with it being almost 11 p.m. But we were happy to have any communication at this point. But as abruptly as the communication began, it stopped.

I tweaked some settings on the Odd Box. One of the

more important things I changed was I changed the box to feed us any words that came over in reverse. This was so anything that came over organically from a radio station was not mistaken as communication because of the computer chip inside this attachment to the box. So a "yes" from a radio station would sound like "say." Imagine playing a record backwards, and everything sounds jumbled; that was what anything broadcast would sound like.

And then I began specifically asking for the spirits that had been reported there on so many occasions, John and Richard. And again, no spirit communication. So Clayton started with the REM pod again. He said, "You know we have a REM pod." And the entire crew busted out laughing. And cracking up, I asked the spirits, "Is it broken? Is the REM pod broken?" And I let them know we just honestly needed verification at this point. And the Odd Box clear as day said, "Yes." Which was a start. We'd figure out how to fix the REM pod later.

But the lines of communication were opened back up, and we needed to keep them open. I then asked, "So who are we chatting with here?" And the Wonder Box said, "John." And this was the guy, the guy who was known for saying rude comments to so many female investigators.

I said, "Hey, John, how come you call all the ladies bad words in here, mean names?" And I said it like it was an honest question, and it was, there was no screaming, there was no yelling. I talked to John like he was there in the room with me. I treat spirits like I would people in real life, and sometimes even better. Then John responded, and we heard the Wonder Box say, "SLUT." But I don't let it get to me. I responded right back with, "Slut, yeah, what's up with that? Did you have a woman break your heart?"

We got nothing from the Odd Box, so I said, "Did your wife cheat on you? Is that why you have no respect for women?" And a loud booming, "YES!" came over again. I was thrilled that he was communicating, that he was telling us his story, that the name-calling had stopped. I told John that I was sorry that happened, and that it didn't mean all women were bad. And then he said, "SLUT," again. I took it as he was calling his wife a slut, because it is possible.

So I told this unseen spirit who was giving us such amazing EVPs, "Let's tell the whole world about your slut wife. Let's get the word out." But I couldn't do that without a name, so I asked John, "What's her name?" After a brief period of time, a name came over, the name Penny. And then the voice stopped. We asked several more questions, trying to find out more about John and why he was there, and he didn't answer a single question. We still weren't feeling any evil, negative or malevolent vibes. None of us were touched. And even when John came over, he wasn't aggressive or threatening in any way. So we decided to give it a break for a bit, and I would return myself later in the evening for a solo investigation.

We got some amazing activity in the upstairs, but the whole time I couldn't wait to go back and do my solo investigation in the warehouse. Again, we had some amazing activity, but all I could think of was how to handle John and how to get him to talk to me. I didn't even care what he told me at that point. We'd gotten to the bottom of why he treated women so horribly, so now I just wanted to know more about him. Why was that room so known for violet activity? I had to get to the bottom of things.

Was I little uneasy? Yeah, I'll admit it, I hate solo investigations. It takes me back to that first Lake County Jail experience just enough to have my senses on alert. But I hate showing on the outside how uneasy I am.

I walked into the fully lit room, I set all my equipment down, and I headed to turn off the lights. I asked both spirits that were known to be there, "Is this what you've been waiting for, boys? You've got me all to yourself now."

Then as I was getting settled in to a nice comfy rolling office-type chair, I asked them to, "Show me what you're made of, boys," with zero hesitation in my voice. If it was going to get crazy in here, I was gonna document the entire thing on video. At the beginning of the evening, our tour guide had shown us around and told us what kind of paranormal activity had happened in each room. And in this room, he was very clear that you had to be aggressive to get any activity. Which we now knew was not true. We did get John to tell us why he hated women. But Richard, who for this investigation I'll call Dick, had not made an appearance yet.

Now we know at this point, I'm not a screamer, I can be a whiner from time to time, but I don't yell at the ghosts unless it's to tell them to chill out and just talk. So instead I get snarky, because honestly that's who I am. And I sat alone, in this dark empty warehouse, with a camera pointed at me on a tripod off in the distance, and one in my hand pointed directly at my face (because that makes better TV), another GoPro about ten feet from the tripod the left, the Odd Box to my side, turned off, on a stack of cardboard boxes filled with newspaper printing supplies, and I said, "I understand John's got some mommy issues going on."

I quickly scanned the room for any movement or shadow play. There was nothing that I could see. So I said, "I just feel like there's nothing going on in this place, like you guys don't have enough balls to bring it out for me," the whole time slowly spinning in my chair while watching the LCD screen for what may or may not pop up behind me. The silence was almost deafening. And no movement that I could see anywhere.

Now one of these two spirits was supposed to be a rather large shadow man as well, and I pulled back to the first investigation back at Lake County Jail, and I decided to flirt with Dick. I mean, what could go wrong? Well, a whole hell of a lot could, but I had a good feeling about this. So I asked Dick if he was the tall shadow figure that was seen at the location, and then I threw out a little, "I've got a thing for tall men." Yep, I did. And then I asked him to show himself to me.

I taunted them a little more and said, "You can't give me a sound, a voice, or a shadow?"

Nothing, so I asked them, "Do I need to give you my spirit box so you can talk to me?" And I did. I mean, why not? It worked earlier in the night, why wouldn't it work again? Even if it was just John who was the only one who communicated again, that was all I really wanted. So I set it up the exact same way and specifically asked to speak to Richard (hoping he liked this better). And I started my questioning. "Richard, are you here? Why are you so angry?" And I kid you not, a voice came over, saying, "He likes you." I asked back, "Richard, you like me?" And a strong response of "YES" came over the Odd Box.

Not gonna lie, the smirk on my face was pretty epic. It was working, and I didn't feel threatened at all, so I just ran with it. Which is how most of my investigations go; I live in the moment and let things happen naturally. I go in with a plan of "we'll head to this room, and this is what we'll bring," and the spirits usually dictate how things go from there.

With the smirk on my face, I told Richard, "OK, let's have a legit conversation." And then the spirit box turned off completely. This had never happened before and, honestly, hasn't happened since. Was John getting jealous of my conversation with Richard? Was it John who turned off the spirit box? I checked, and it was as if the plug had been pulled out of the spirit box, and like I said, this never happens. Was it John? We'll never know, as no cameras were on the spirit/Odd Box combo at the time. And it drives me crazy to this day.

I turned my attention fully to the box, got it running again, and right away, it said, "Hi," and then it said, "Hello," in two separate voices. As if both of them were with me now. There was distinctly another voice coming through now. I asked Richard how old he was, and he without hesitation said, "Forty." I then asked, "Can you show yourself to any of the cameras in the room with me?" and right away the box said in the same voice that said forty, "NO." And then I said, "Can you tell me your last name, Richard?" And as quickly as the first two responses came, it said, "I can't."

I was feeling really good about picking the creepy room for this solo investigation and leaving the boys in the alleged brothel.

I was having a legit conversation, no threats, no name-calling; it felt really good to me. This same warehouse was known for one more spirit, and they call him the cowboy. He's benign, he doesn't really interact, but he's seen from time to time. So I asked, either spirit at this point, "Who's the cowboy?" The response over the spirit box was as if both were answering but at separate times. They said, "Eric," you know, like I should know that already. They both said it so matter-of-fact like. Do different spirits in the same location know each other? Do they hang out? That was how I took the same response in two different voices. It was like they thought I should know him because I was there. It was exhilarating.

And as I was processing this all in my head, the word "beautiful" came over the Odd Box. Ummm, OK, here I thought I was walking into a den of evil, and they were complimenting me. In all seriousness, this was refreshing and exciting, and compliments will get you everywhere with me, but my guard was still up. If these spirits were responsible for all the chaos on previous investigations, there had to be a reason. I mean, to me the guys seemed swell.

And the buttering up didn't stop there. I kept talking to them conversationally, and then what I was pretty sure was John said, "I think you're pretty." I thanked him for the compliment, and then the word "beautiful" came over again. I mean, come on, guys, I'm blushing. I thanked these unseen men again and asked them, "Which one of you just called me beautiful?" And immediately the Odd Box said, "Dick." I mean, come on, this was literally the perfect spirit box session in my eyes.

With all these compliments, I brought up Jeff, the gentleman who gave us the tour and who runs all the investigations at the Herald. I flat out asked, "Do you like Jeff?" And the box repeated Jeff's name. I then asked if they had any messages for him. And they then said what sounded like, in unison, "Get out." And I didn't think they meant me. I thought that was the message they wanted me to relay to Jeff. I then asked them, "Do you want Jeff to get out, or do you want me to get out?" Because if they were talking to me, (1) I wasn't getting out, and (2) my feelings might get hurt a little. But the response was just as I thought it was, they said, "Jeff."

Now since these responses were so spot on and so clear, let me remind you that I had a setting on the Wonder Box where any words it might pick up through the spirit box radio were being put into reverse through an amplifier on the Odd Box, so my mind was literally blown.

I asked the spirits if there was anything else they would like to say, when I heard a disembodied voice behind me. I wasn't scared, but was curious. Were they trying to talk to me this way now? But I couldn't quite make out what was said because of the loud static coming over the Odd Box at the time.

And then the voices stopped completely, either in the room or out of the Odd Box. Was that one of the spirits saying goodbye? Trust me, I wish I knew, but I like to think it was. And the room felt a little more empty after that as well. Did they run out of the energy needed to communicate? Did they have an appointment they needed to keep? I had no idea, but I WANTED ANSWERS.

I started packing things up, and as I do at any location, even after communication stops, I thanked them for their time and willingness to communicate and for being so kind.

I did pass the message on to Jeff. And I hope that Jeff made up with John and Dick and that someday I am able to make it back there. Because a girl does love being told she's beautiful. Oh yeah, and get more amazing evidence. But what I learned is that my grandpa Stobbs was one million percent right. If you show someone in a bad mood a little compassion, it goes a long way. And I still use this technique to this day. And I still get some amazing evidence.

Mitchell Opera House, Mitchell, Indiana

MITCHELL OPERA HOUSE is one of the closest investigations we have ever done to my home, so I was thrilled that we were given the opportunity to investigate the place for the very first time. We had to jump through some hoops, but I was so very happy that we did.

The building had been used in many different ways over the years, but it started out as an opera house and had just recently been restored to its former beauty.

There were no real instances of hauntings, but several mediums had been at shows at the Mitchell Opera House and had sensed a few different spirits.

I could not wait to begin and wanted to start in the theater itself. Both Carter and Clayton had seen movement in the balcony as we were setting up, and Carter actually saw his very first spirit apparition before we even turned the lights off. And right after that happened, as I was explaining out loud that this was why we were here, that we wanted this kind of interaction, and I thanked them, I heard a male voice. Not sure what it said, I mistook it for Clayton outside, but we checked, and Clayton wasn't back yet, and at the time, I had no idea what it said. Once I was able to review the iPhone video I had been taking, the spirit was saying, "You're welcome," right after my thanking the spirits. And we knew it was going to be a good night.

We turned off the lights behind the stage and settled into this beautifully restored theater. I was sitting in the theater seats, Carter and Clayton were on the stage, each of us had our own camera, and we had a laser grid point from the stage to the wall where Carter had seen a spirit earlier in the night. A GoPro camera was pointing down toward the stage from the balcony as a static camera, and a camera was constantly surveying the laser grid pointed toward the back of the house.

Clayton started things off with a question we all wanted an answer to: "Did you intentionally show yourself to Carter?" And we waited. Again, this was the very first investigation of the opera house, and we never know what we're going to get when this is the case. Carter had, however, seen an apparition that he explained to be child height. He also said it was almost see-through, and he could only see from the shoulders down. And I heard a voice, and thank everything that is holy, it didn't stop there. We all heard a child's voice in the theater. And it echoed throughout the theater and reverberated. I actually felt it sitting in the theater seats. It was the voice of a small child, and that small child answered Clayton's question with a "yeah."

OK, this is every investigator's wet dream. You witness paranormal activity when you're not even looking yet, and you get a disembodied voice directly answering your very first question, and the entire team hears it. Well, maybe not every investigator's dream, but it is certainly mine. And as Clayton thanked the spirits for interacting with us, the entire crew heard movement in the stairwell leading up to the balcony, the same stairwell Carter had seen the apparition running toward. Oh, it's ON this evening, but we had no idea what we were in store for.

We continued to sit quietly, to see if they would continue to communicate that way, and I heard what sounded like a deep thudding, like someone was running around above my head on the ceiling that is, I'd have to guess, twenty-five feet high at least. At this point, however, a theater was built for different sound than we are used to, so I can't be sure. I, however, was the only one who heard this evidence. The cameras didn't even pick up the sound. I didn't question myself at all, I knew exactly what I'd heard, and I thought it was coming from the balcony.

So we sat quietly for a little longer, and Clayton mentioned that he was hearing a conversation that sounded very faint and very far away, and he couldn't quite make out what was being said, or who was saying it. And I breathed a deep sigh of relief, because I'd been hearing the same thing since I sat out in the theater seats, but I figured if the boys didn't hear the footsteps, they certainly weren't going to hear this, and boy, was I glad I was wrong on that one. To me it sounded like people in the same seating area I was sitting in. And the people in the seats were talking in a hushed tone so as not to be rude to anyone else in the theater. I didn't hear a conversation, but conversations (plural).

Clayton and I decided this was residual energy left behind by the hundreds and hundreds of people who have sat in these seats. There are several kinds of hauntings, but to keep it basic, residual, and intelligent are the two biggies. Like in this situation, that happened so often, this energy left an imprint in time and space. This happens often in places of entertainment, because the energy is so happy, and emotions in theaters are so all over the board while watching a performance. There's no one energy or spirit or ghost attached; residual energy can be left behind by a living person. I'm sure that when I move out of my house, someone may be haunted by the residual energy of me walking back and forth to my coffee maker all day every day.

But intelligent hauntings are of a soul, a specific energy, a spirit left behind, that can interact with you, just like the child answering yes to Clayton's question asking if the energy had meant to show itself, and we all heard the response "yes" clear as day. And I won't lie, intelligent hauntings are my favorite, and that's why I do this. But a place like this, it makes sense to have both kinds of hauntings going on at once. Theaters and schools are some of the most haunted locations across the board. And I would have to say in my personal experience, jails and prisons run a close third.

And thank goodness our intelligent friends were right back. I heard a voice again, a child's voice, say Sara, and right after I mentioned this to the boys, and they said they did not hear it, Clayton saw movement in the back of the house, and as he was explaining it, I realized he was explaining exactly what Carter had seen, doing the exact same thing, and even though the laser grid was facing that way, nothing was captured on that static camera. But I believe they both saw this. I have no doubt. And he saw it heading in the same direction. Was that what I heard, these children running around in the balcony? No solid evidence pointed that way, but it made sense.

I then heard shuffling feet behind me, in the same area both Clayton and Carter saw something. And then both Clayton and I heard a young child's voice again. This time we couldn't make out what it said, but it sounded like it was having a good time. Was it children playing? Were these the sounds we were hearing, and what was being seen? Were THEY observing us? Talk about a plot twist.

We took a brief break to grab some more equipment and bring it out, and we all headed to the back of the house where all the activity was happening. We brought our SLS camera, which is a camera hooked up to the old X-Box Kinect, which reads the area it's pointed at by emitting hundreds maybe thousands of little lasers that you can't see with the naked eye, and tries to find human-shaped entities, as well as just plain humans. When it registers a human-shaped figure, it shows up on the tablet attached to it as a stick figure. This is a newer piece of equipment, and we hadn't had a whole lot of luck with it so far.

We also brought out the Odd Box, and this time decided to hook it up to a tablet instead of the spirit box. The tablet has an app on it we've had great success with over the years. This app has prerecorded voices on it, three different voices, a male, a female, and a child. And the voices just play randomly in no specific order, and the voices all speak in reverse, so nothing makes sense. The spirits are said to manipulate the voices on this app, just as they can on a spirit box. I accidentally had it attached at an investigation, and totally forgot the Odd Box was set to reverse everything that came over, and we thought we were crazy because we could understand everything that was being said, until I figured out my mistake. But this app works for paranormal investigations just like the spirit box does. It's said that the spirits can manipulate the voices and use the sound to say what they want. It's been very interesting as well, female entities use the female voice, males use the male voice, and children use the child's voice. Do I know why? No, but it's pretty damn cool. It's an amazing app; it's called Portal Plus. I also have a K2 meter in my hand. And we all have our respective cameras in hand.

I asked any spirit to interact with us by using their energy to make the K2 meter in my hand light up. And I felt something touch my hand for a moment, not a grab or a scratch, it was similar to the feeling of a feather gently swiping my hand. However, the K2 meter did not light up at all. So as I set the gray box down on the floor, I said, "Do you not want to get that close to me?" And there was an immediate response from the female voice saying, "No!" I then walked to the stairs that had seen so much activity earlier in the evening and walked away. I then put a static camera facing the K2 meter on the stairs.

As I was walking away, Clayton asked me to come over and see what he had on the SLS camera. When I got there, I was so excited. We had finally captured something on the new device. It looked like a small child, smaller than both Clayton and Carter had seen earlier in the evening, trying to peek over a chair in the last row of seats in the theater. I mean, all its little stick-figure parts were there, with its hands on the back of the chair, looking over it. And this was near where I was just standing. Was the stick figure I was now looking at what had touched me just moments earlier? And then we heard the child's voice say, "I don't see them nowhere." Did he lose sight of us? Was he looking for someone else? I couldn't wait to find out. But as soon as he showed up in our SLS camera, he disappeared almost as fast.

Immediately after the apparition disappeared, the child's voice came over even clearer this time and said, "You'll see it?" Were these two children talking to each other, or was it just the same child giving himself a pep talk? And then the child's voice spoke again through the Odd Box with no questions asked, as our concentration was pretty firmly on the SLS camera and trying to capture more evidence. "But what he says is both adorable and concerning," the voice said. "It's very spooky."

We then turned our full attention to the voice communicating with us. I asked, "Do we scare you?"

And a female voice came over the box immediately, saying, "Yeah." But it was a long drawn-out yeah.

We decided to split up and spread out a bit within the seats. I never want to overcrowd an entity. We're in their space, we are there asking them to communicate, surely overcrowding them, and scaring them isn't the way to go about it. So each of us headed to a different area in the seats to continue this conversation with the other side.

As we were settling in, the child's voice came over and started questioning us. He asked, "Do you see us?" And I immediately responded, "I don't see you, but I'd like to." And then we heard a noise as we were discussing it. The Odd Box said in the adult male's voice, "Outside." And things were starting to click. He was telling us where the noises were coming from. I thought at this point they WERE investigating us. It was like he was saying out loud that he'd heard something outside, like we do, so in review we don't mistake it for paranormal. Then that same man's voice said, "Turn around." We were all at this point looking toward the front of the house, as that's the way the seats are pointed. And just moments later, Clayton heard footsteps directly behind us.

This was all amazing evidence, but it's never enough for me, so I asked the man who'd been speaking if he can tell us his name, to kind of take it back to us investigating them. And the next three words that came over would solidify who we were speaking to. First it said, "Dave," in a whisper that could have been either the male or the female. Then we heard, in that same whisper, "David," and then in the male's voice we clearly heard, "I'm David," and he followed up with a, "How's that?" and I answered, "David, that's amazing."

I needed to know more about this man. I asked, "David, did you work here?" And that same voice replied, "I was talent." Was this spirit a performer from back in the vaudeville days? Just as abruptly as it started, it stopped again, so we decided to call it quits in the theater itself for the evening. But this specific investigation of the theater at the Mitchell Opera House was the first time and only time my team has been investigated by the spirits that reside at a location. And it was magical.

Fear Factory, Salt Lake City, Utah

I HAD SEEN an investigation of this place on TV, and it was intense to say the least. The location was an old cement factory that had been there for over a decade and was turned into a haunted attraction. There's a big difference between a haunted location and a haunted attraction. A haunted attraction is open to the public every fall up until Halloween, the place is decorated to be creepy, and actors are inside to scare people. But this haunted attraction is also a haunted location, because we were here to find paranormal activity in February in the frigid cold. Now that's dedication.

Anyway, back to the TV show, the team claimed that the silos at this location had a demon summoned there, and said demon is still there taunting everyone who enters. OK, sure. This show also tends to find demons at most of their locations, and as you know, I personally don't happen to believe there are demons running around on Earth, so when I heard we were heading to SLC for work, I talked to a friend there who knew the people who ran Fear Factory, and I was able to schedule an overnight investigation. I was stoked, and yeah, a little nervous. I mean, I certainly didn't want to find out I was wrong about my stance on demons in the freezing cold in a huge metal silo in Utah, am I right? I sure hoped so.

So we bundled up, packed up our equipment, and flew out to Salt Lake City, which has now become one of my favorite places in the country. We got our meetings done, and Clayton and I had horrible head colds from the travel. But we bundled up like we've never done before and put 666 west and 800 south into the GPS and headed over from our hotel.

As we drove in, the place was MASSIVE, and this girl, being so in love with all things industrial, was one happy camper. I mean, this place was too cool for demons to hang out, right? Again I had a pit at the bottom of my stomach. What if this place really was infested with demons? What if what I'd based my whole investigative career on proving was really just my opinion this whole time? Was tonight the night I changed my stance on demons and possession? These were the thoughts that were running through my head. Maybe it was because I was sick, but I was more worried than I usually am when going into a place known for aggressive spirits, aka demons.

We started the investigation elsewhere, but our second stop was what I was currently calling the "demon silo." We had placed an order for pizza delivery before we headed in, because I was thinking we'd be in and out with no evidence. I'm just gonna tell you now, I was wrong.

We went in with cameras galore, the Odd Box, and the SLS camera. On this trip Clayton had brought his boyfriend, James, along. And it's always fun when he's there. Carter worked on getting the SLS camera up and running, I got the Odd Box set up, and Clayton and James worked on our static cameras.

The vibe in this place was strange; your balance just felt a little off. However, after discussing it with the crew, we decided it was the fact that we were in a ginormous circle made out of metal, no insulation at all, and with the highway right next to this silo, the sounds were making us feel a little off balance.

Once everything was set up, I grabbed the SLS camera, and I started our introduction like we do at every location. I let them know, like always, we were there out of love, light, peace, and positivity. And that we were there to talk to the spirits of the same love, light, peace, and positivity. I let them know we were not there to hurt them, harm them, yell at them, or take them away, and we added to that we actually WANTED them to stay there. And then I explained our equipment to them, you know, like there weren't any demons there. There were a few more ums in the intro than usual, not sure if it was the cold and sinus medication I was on, or if it was fear. But if you ask me, I'll totally say the cold meds.

As I finished the explanation of the SLS camera I was holding, and turned to look at it, there was a damn stick figure straight off the bat, standing on a faux rock right in front of me. It was small, and I asked it to raise its hand if it could hear me, and watching the tablet screen, I saw the stick figure raise both of its arms above its head. And then the stick figure brought its arms back down and crossed them over its chest, and then it simply disappeared. This figure didn't bring with it any bad feelings in the silo. This spirit just showed up for a moment, as if to say, hey, we're here, don't discount the silo and order pizza delivery. Oooops, my bad.

The silo, as I stated, was so loud we couldn't do any EVP sessions with a digital recorder. The sounds of the highway would drown out the most clear EVPs. So I went next right to my favorite piece of equipment, the

Odd Box. I set the SLS camera on the rock I had just been standing next to, and I went to dig out the Odd Box from my carry-on luggage. Because we fancy like that. And as I brought the Odd Box out, I saw the stick figure was back on the SLS camera, for only a second and a half. I thought whatever was in this demon silo, aside from us, was ready to talk. So I quickly got things out and set up as fast as I could.

While I was doing this, Clayton was trying to figure out where the stick figure was standing when the camera captured it, and it wasn't on the rock I thought it was, it was floating in the air. And while Clayton was standing there showing me where it would have been, he felt a large presence behind him, and he didn't say he was uncomfortable, but I could see it in his eyes. Just as I was trying to read his body language, I felt a touch on my right side, right at my waist. I was pretty bundled up, two shirts on, a sweatshirt and a full down-filled winter coat. But it felt like it was a full hand touching me under my coat and on top of my sweatshirt. I felt a full hand at my waistline; if it was a cold hand, I honestly wouldn't know, it was a balmy 25 degrees in the silo that night. What I felt, however, was the pressure. All the while, Clayton was trying to get the stick figure to appear again next to him on the SLS camera, sadly to no avail.

I finished getting the Odd Box set up and hooked it up to the spirit box. Before we could even settle into start our questions, a loud and clear, "Hi there!" came over the spirit box. OK, either this demon was polite as hell, or it was like I thought, these spirits were ready to communicate. The spirit box again said, "Hi," and I let my guard down for the night and said, "Hi, how are you? Can you tell us your name?" And the same male voice that said "hi there" said, "Go on," and then a female voice we were hearing for the very first time said, "Linda." We had names, and it was absolutely not Lord of Hellfire. No demons here, people.

We continued, and I asked how many people were in this silo right now. And we instantly got a younger female voice saying, "Five," and there were only four of us of the living at the time in the silo. Did she mean herself and us? And then we got the most bizarre response to the question asking whom we were speaking with. The Wonder Box replied, totally fluid in a female voice, "Bob snitched on me." Now this plant had been abandoned for quite some time before it became Fear Factory, and during this time several homeless people had moved into the outlying buildings. Could this be someone who was killed or died of exposure during that time? We found out during our tour, several people took their lives on the railroad tracks just outside the fenced-in area of Fear Factory, and one of those instances was no less than three months earlier than when I was there. Could it be one of those poor people who took their own lives just steps away from the property line? Could Bob have told of something so horrific that the person who committed the act of suicide just couldn't see any other way out?

I was so intrigued at this point. Then the spirit box in two different voices just beats apart said, "Kitsie," and, "Run." I was not having it. And I firmly said, "We're just here to communicate. You're not going to scare me by telling me to run." And then a female voice came over: "I'm serious," in a very motherly tone, like when you were a kid and in trouble for doing something, and your mom would tell you to stop, and you did it again. Then she came back with, "I'm serious."

I decided to put away the SLS camera since we hadn't captured any stick figures that weren't us for quite some time. And I really wanted to focus on this very odd communication going on with the Odd Box.

So I asked a simple question, "Can you see us?" To which the response was quick and from a male voice, saying, very matter-of-fact, "I can see you." And then in the same male voice, a loud and clear, "Look at you," boomed out of the box.

And that was when the pizza-delivery person called Clayton to meet him outside the gate. He and James headed out to get the pizza. And Carter and I stayed to find out as much as we could about the not so demon-like spirits in the silo before their energy depleted. After they were out of the silo, I turned the Odd Box back on. The first question I asked was, "Is there anything you want to tell us?" To which I got no response. So I gave it a minute and said, "Any messages you want us to tell the world?" And a few beats later, a very deep male voice came over and said, "Here it goes." Mind you, there was no tension or negative energy felt in the silo at all. I replied what I think anyone would, "Here what goes?" And it WENT!

We got several responses right in a row, for ten to twenty seconds straight, several different voices said "devil" and "demon" over and over again. And I was NOT having it. Demons schmeamons. Like I said, not a negative ounce of energy in the air. I decided to put my foot down, so to speak, and I responded with, "I feel like you keep saying devil and demon just to freak us out. It's not freaking me out at all," and I kept going, I put on my mommy voice and said, "I feel like you've been trained to do this here, not intentionally, but people come here looking for that, and you give them what they want. I want to know your real name." And there were several more questions asked with no response. But I finally asked, "Can I bribe you with pizza?" And we got the immediate response from that deep male voice who said "here it goes." But this time he said, "That could work." Has bribing a spirit with pizza ever been done before? Well, let's see if it works here.

So I've had this burning question since I started using the Odd Box. I used to use it at home A LOT when I first got it. And I had it long before Anna followed me home, and I would get responses from spirits I knew weren't in my house. Sometimes I would use it to ask questions about upcoming investigations, and I would get information that would come to fruition. Like Anna herself.

I asked the question to the box, "Is this thing that you're talking through now a portal? And if so, where are you speaking from now?" And the response blew my mind. The box said in a female voice I was becoming familiar with, "Heaven." At this point my thoughts were confirmed, but I had no idea how much so until a different female voice came over and said, "Nebraska." And then a male voice came over and said, "London," but with a very American accent. I still to this day don't know for sure if it's a portal, but that evidence is pretty compelling, don't you think?

I then specifically asked the female voice that we had been talking to pretty much since we turned the box on for her name. And the name "Linda" came over. But it wasn't her voice. I then asked, "Why are you still here?" And a male voice came over and blew my mind. He said, "Where do you expect me to be?" And the female voice came over and said MY NAME.

OK, spirits, let's do this, let's hear your story. I then asked whoever would answer me, "Are you stuck here? Do you want to leave here?" And the female voice, who I was assuming was Linda at this point, told me, "No chance to leave." WOW. And then she said, "I don't."

I started getting the feeling they wanted me to help

them leave, whether it be to move to whatever is on the other side, or just anywhere else but here. But I always let spirits know that I personally can't cross them over. Yeah, I can tell them to look for the light, to find family members and join them, I guess. But I don't REALLY know, so I don't. My biggest fear is that I'll try and fail miserably, and there'll be some spirit of a brothel gal stuck in a daycare for eternity. I just won't do it. So I let them know, "I can't send you anywhere else."

And then Clayton and James made their way back in. They put the pizza in the oven in the lunchroom to keep it warm, because they knew there were stories to be told in this place too. I couldn't wait to tell them about the latest developments with Linda and crew.

Once I filled the boys in on what had happened in their absence, we got right back into it. Clayton asked, "Do you feel like you have to pretend to be the devil or Satan to get people out of here?" And he explained his theory to me after asking the question. Explained that he wondered if the spirits were just trying to give investigators what they wanted to hear, just so they could be left alone. Which made total sense to me. None of us had felt any energy that alerted us in any way, and the fact that after I called them out on the devil and demon shit, it stopped. And ever since, it had been legit communication, some of the best we had ever had. And I started wondering out loud if maybe the spirits here were just bored, and playing demon was a form of entertainment for them. And before I could finish completing my last sentence, a male voice came over loud and clear, saying, "They want it." WHOA. This just confirmed Clayton's thoughts. The spirits were acting like "demons" because that was what the people who came in here wanted. MIND BLOWN. An intelligent haunting having an intelligent conversation, this was amazing.

Well, an amazing potty-mouth intelligent conversation, because a younger female voice came over and said, "That bitch done it," or, "That bitch Donna." So Donna, if you're reading this, sorry. But was she putting the blame on one person? Are these spirits trapped here to entertain the masses? Were these spirits bound here by someone? Was witchcraft used at some point? The spirits were opening up to us, and I couldn't be happier, but now I was feeling so bad for them at the same time. Hopefully we could find out more about this. I was hoping nothing had been done to force these spirits here for pure entertainment value.

I then asked a question that I usually never do. I really try to keep religion out of this. But if a spirit was religious in life, like the one who said she was in heaven, maybe it might help this time around. I asked the spirits if anyone was in purgatory, and Linda's voice came over again, so clear that it was like she was standing in front of the Odd Box, and she said, "I am." And just after we got that response, I saw across from where I was standing a misty smokey humanoid figure staying just outside our circle, and just watching us, just behind James. And when I mentioned it to the boys, James told me, "I've been feeling like there's someone over here." The area I'm speaking of was a dead end and set dressed to look like a cave, so there was no way anyone could be in that area without us knowing it. As soon as I saw the misty figure, it disappeared. I hoped my calling it out didn't make it want to leave.

We worked on debunking what I had seen with maybe car lights, or anything of the sort, but we were in a silo with no windows. We just couldn't find a way to explain it as a natural occurrence. And as we were finishing up, Clayton saw shadow movement where we were just standing, and this time we were fortunate to get it on camera. And it wasn't really shaped like anything, but Clayton described it best. He said he saw, "A shift of overall darkness," that just started halfway into the frame and then slid off to the left and disappeared into the haunt set. So what we had here was I saw a light smokey figure on one side of all of us, and Clayton saw a darkness on the opposite side of us. Not feeling threatened at all, but wanting to know more, Clayton asked the Odd Box, "Did you just come up on either side of us?" and the Odd Box seemed to boom, "We did."

My theory is this, the spirits that are in this silo are seeing that others are communicating with us, and I'm sure many more have stories to tell, and they would like us to tell them. But we only have so much time left in our investigation, and we need to come up with a plan of attack. I chose to focus on the Odd Box. I needed to find out why these spirits were here, and why they felt they had to perform.

I then let them know that it was OK, that we weren't scared, that this was exactly what we wanted. And we wanted to communicate with them and would love to see more of them. And Linda came over the Odd Box, saying, "I don't think she does." We laughed it off.

I then asked Linda, "Who all are you speaking for?" And her quick response was, "Many." But at the time, I thought she had said twenty. This happens every once in a while, where I think one thing is said, and upon evidence review, it's something completely different, and I'm like DERP. So Clayton asked, "Are there twenty of you?" And a male voice came over, saying, "Five," and when he said it, his words almost reverberated through the room, and I literally felt it in my soul. These spirits didn't want us thinking there were twenty of them there and wanted us to know it was just five. And we wouldn't make that mistake again.

But we were curious, since it had said there were five of us earlier (and again there are only four people in our group, but five if you included Anna, the spirit from the Culbertson mansion, who came along from time to time), did it mean us, or five of them? So we asked what they meant, and the response was, "Five people." And it almost sounded like two people were saying it at once. And then a female voice said, "And behind you is six." Wait, WHAT? They had to be talking about themselves at this point, because no person with a beating heart was behind us, unless they were wearing the cloak of Invisibility. But then Linda came through, with a tone of heartache, and said, "We are just people." And mystery solved, they were the people, and there were six of them there. And the way she said it almost broke my heart. Once I realized what she said, I started tearing up and was totally taken aback. In those four little words, in that tone, it told me so much. It was like she was answering two questions in one. We knew now how many of them there were, and the way she said it came across like, stop treating us like we're evil, stop making us perform, treat us like people, because we are just people.

This was a HUGE revelation for the paranormal community and verified so much of what I had been feeling since the beginning. Investigators NEED to start treating these spirits they pay so much money to investigate like they would a neighbor, like they would a friend, like they would a family member. Stop yelling at the entities, stop asking them to do tricks for you, treat them like they are people and they will talk to you, they will tell you their story. We should do this in our personal lives too. Everybody stop being an asshole.

OK, I'm stepping off my soapbox, and back to the investigation at hand. I let these people who are no longer on the earthly plane know how appreciative we were for their communication, that we were so happy they chose us to tell their story to. And James let them know we were just there to have fun, that we were not there to make them out to be something they were not.

The next word that came over was very important: "ask." I then questioned if they wanted us to tell the investigators to stop yelling at them, and three words came over from two different spirits, "definitely" and "absolutely" and "yeah." I promised Linda and the crew I would let the people who run the location know. And Clayton told them all, "If you don't want to perform for people as the devil and demons, don't. You can simply just sit silent." And what came over next, (1) let us know that they were done for the night, and (2) was the sweetest send-off we've ever gotten on any investigation. Linda came through and said, "It's late, sweetheart." And we said our goodbyes, and when we were done, a male voice asked us, "Leaving?" And we let them know that we were.

This investigation taught me so much, and I hope it teaches so many the same. So, from Linda and the crew at the demon silo at Fear Factory in Salt Lake City, Utah, treat everyone with respect, especially the ones you can't see.

CHAPTER 3

BOBBY MACKEY'S

*B*obby Mackey's is a country bar, or honky-tonk, in Northern Kentucky, just outside Cincinnati, Ohio. It's an oddly shaped building built on a hill. You'd never know just driving by that in the paranormal world, this location is said to be haunted by aggressive demons. There are so many stories, and just about every paranormal cable show has done an investigation here. People claim they have become addicted to drugs after investigating the place. Tall stories for a harmless little building on an old country road. This place has been cleansed so many times by clergy that it should be fit to perform a baptism in. Yet the stories still keep coming, and the claims get bigger and bigger. And Clayton had actually refused to investigate this place due to the claims. Until one day he turned to me and said, "Ya know, let's investigate Bobby Mackey's." As you can guess, I looked at him like he was crazy, but quickly booked it for and investigation before he could change his mind.

Let me tell you a little bit about the lore of this place. When the namesake Bobby Mackey bought it, he had a handyman living on-site; his name was Carl Lawson. He lived above the honky-tonk. This has been documented on several paranormal TV shows with interviews of all involved. I will preface this with Bobby himself does not believe in ghosts. But his wife and handyman did. One day the wife was working on getting the place ready for opening, and she felt like she was pushed down the stairs by an evil force. And not long after that Carl became effected and felt like something was trying to possess him. So much so that a priest was brought in and did an exorcism on Carl. There's a bit more, but nothing relevant to the story. Later Carl died on January 26, 2012, at the early age of fifty-four. His death had nothing to do with the haunting. Carl was interviewed many times over the years about his experience at Bobby Mackey's.

Yep, you know me well enough by now to know I pretended like I wasn't around the crew, but I was more nervous than I had ever been on an investigation before. The stories about this place, which I'm sure are completely exaggerated, were a lot for one little investigator to take in. It had recently been proved that the main legend and very prominent haunting of a female, who had been said to have killed herself here, had not happened at all. And that story and the demons in the basement were I all I had ever known about the place. And since we know I can't imagine if demons are real, they certainly wouldn't be haunting some honky-tonk in Wilder, Kentucky, I had no idea who might be haunting this place. So after the tour, we learned that this place was a mobster hot spot back in the '20s and '30s. And mobsters, as we know, are my JAM. I am a true crime junkie, who grew up right outside Chicago; how can I not be? OK, enough about the prequel to our investigation, let's get on to the good stuff. And the good stuff started off fast and hard, just like I like it. But I was not anticipating it at all.

It was July 3, so we had to be careful that fireworks weren't mistaken for paranormal activity, and it was a scorcher that day, and unbeknownst to us, they turn all the air-conditioning units off at night, and when it's hot at a location, we always head up as far as we can go to get the hottest part over with first.

It was a small apartment with a small living space where we were investigating tonight. The room separated by wall studs, with no walls attached to them, and a bar at the far end. We were in Carl's room, but it was also what used as a gambling den back in the days the mobsters ruled the Midwest. It was so cool, there was a little hidden door buzzer at the bottom of the stairs that was left behind, and not many people know about it. Of course, I had to be THAT girl before we headed up, and press the buzzer to let anyone up there know we were on our way. So let's get to it so we can get out of there.

This investigation crew was me, my right-hand man Clayton, my son Carter, and James came along for this one too. We settled in, cameras were set up, equipment was out, and I started telling the spirits upstairs our intentions, just like every other investigation. I got the Odd Box set up, and the batteries in the spirit box were completely drained. This had never happened before; the batteries were drained before I had even turned it on. And I had just replaced the batteries before we went upstairs. Within the paranormal community, it's said that spirits can drain batteries of all their energy in order to use it for communication or manifesting. So, needless to say, I was hopeful from the get-go.

The entire crew got a light-headed feeling up in what was Carl's apartment during the setup, but we couldn't decide if it was the heat or paranormal; it was honestly a toss-up. But I personally did get a very heavy feeling of being watched. Which does happen quite often, with good reason too. I mean, we're in their space, we can tell them we mean them no harm, but they want us to prove it, and we're always happy to do so. And I was ready to do so. So now loaded with fresh batteries again, I started up the Odd Box attached to the spirit box. We always started out with the spirit box, and if there was no activity, moved on to a couple of different apps that are available.

Thank goodness it fired up this time. I explained to the spirits that it was a portal of sorts (thanks to Linda from Fear Factory for that confirmation), and it was the easiest way for us to have a real-time conversation with any soul that wished to speak to us. I was oh so very hopeful for communication right off the bat, and secretly hoping I wasn't wrong on my whole stance on demons.

Almost immediately a voice came over and said, "Hi, Kits," and another said, "Carter." And there you have it, immediate intelligent communication. And we hadn't asked a single question yet. Let's hope things continued. I still hadn't had a chance to ask a single question yet, and a male voice came over with a Southern drawl and an unadulterated clarity with a slower cadence. The voice said, "Let me... talk... to 'em." And I kid you not, it was the voice of Carl Larson. I had heard that voice so many times; it was unmistakable.

Clayton then asked, "Carl, are you here with us?" And another deeper, more throaty male voice came out of the box, saying, "No, you won't." This does happen sometimes, we get communication, and some other spirit doesn't let them talk. I was a little heartbroken, I did want to talk more to Carl, but this was the card we were dealt. And then a bunch of nothing came over. I have no idea how the hierarchy of a haunted location works, but it would seem there was someone there who didn't want Carl communicating with us, which was such a bummer, because we were off to such a good start. We kept asking questions, and nothing really definitive or that made any sense to the question we were asking came over the Odd Box.

So then Clayton said, "We know a lot of people come here, a lot of people probably ask you the exact same questions, but we aren't those people." He was looking directly at the Odd Box as he said, "We want you to tell your story, your true story, not another story that other people have made up. Just your true story. How many people are here?"

A few moments after that, we heard a younger female voice, or so we thought, say, "I'm running away." And a male voice said, "Again?"

Clayton then asked, "Who is the female? Can you tell us your name?" And I confirmed that we only wanted to speak to the female. I was completely intrigued. Why was she running away? Who was she running away from? And she responded again, the same voice, asking us, "What do you want?" She sounded hesitant. And I assumed it was the same girl who said she was running away, or she had a voice twin. She sounded kind of annoyed as well. So it appeared we had a sassy spirit on our hands, and I mean, you know I can outsass any spirit.

I started off encouraging. I let them know we just

wanted to communicate, that we weren't going to yell or threaten them in any way. And then I heard the same female voice say, "Coming." And just a few beats later a male voice said, "Leave," very sternly. Don't worry, we weren't intimidated at all. Oh, you weren't, good, that means you've been paying attention.

Then, at just that moment, I saw the most amazing thing I had ever seen in a very long time. I saw a head-shaped glowing light, white in color, peek its way around the corner and duck back out. I was so stunned all I could say out loud was SHHHHHHHHHHHHHH-HHH. Words had a hard time coming to me. The crew was staring at me, asking me what was wrong. I was still trying to process what I had just seen. All I could do was point at the door, breathing heavily. And after stuttering and stammering a bit with unnatural pauses, I said, "It was like a head, like a glowing head leaning over to look around the corner of the door to peek in and lean back out." And the response I got from Clayton was, "Seriously?" And I responded in a high-pitched almost laughing voice, "Seriously. In the fucking doorway right there. I'm not even kidding right now." I never get when the internet trolls say things like, "Come on, you're looking for the ghosts. Why are you so freaked out when things happen?" And I'm gonna say to those assholes, you do it, and when you see one, you'll piss your pants.

And that voice, that same voice, came over the spirit box and said, "Abby."

I asked, "Abby, was that you?"

She responded, "Maybe." I already liked her.

So I asked her to come on in, and explained to her that I wasn't scared or mad, that I was just very excited to meet her. And fuck yeah, I was. Come on in with your glowing self, girl! But Clayton wasn't feeling that at all and told me, "I'm a little scared."

Ok, let me tell you more about what our cameras captured. It was more than I even saw. So, bonus. What we captured with the infrared camera Clayton was holding was a light anomaly that looks like an arm coming out and grabbing the doorway from behind, and then ever so slowly you see another light anomaly shaped like a head peek out from behind the wall the doorway was attached to. And much faster than peeking in, it ducked back out, head first, and then the arm. And this all happened right after the female voice had said, "Coming," over the Odd Box and the male voice followed up with, "Leave." I don't think the male voice was talking to us at all, but was talking to the apparition I had just seen. And she followed up this amazing event by finally telling us her name. We were dealing with a spirit named Abby.

We were on the second floor of the building, all windows were covered and sealed, and the doorway had a small landing before walking in, and was stairs the rest of the way down. There is no window at the top of the stairs. There is no way this could be outside light contamination, especially since this light was coming in from outside the door. This whole room was very dusty, that would have to be one hell of a dust bunny, and add the fact that I saw this light with my own eyes, we definitely had something paranormal going on. And now I needed to know more.

I finally calmed down a little and asked Abby to come to where my voice was, reassuring her that it was OK and we didn't want to hurt her. I again told her I was so excited to meet her. And Carter deciphered the next voice that came over the Odd Box next. He heard, "I'm nervous." I then felt the overwhelming urge to reassure her in a way that was lighthearted and hopefully a little funny. I said, "I may have resting bitch face, but I'm not a bitch."

I told the boys I hadn't seen anything like this since Ferry Plantation. Ferry still holds the top spot for my most detailed ghost sighting, but this I will take. I felt a female presence, and then the box said Abby. As I was speaking to the boys, the box said hello in a different voice. I again let them know we were not here to hurt or harm them, or even yell at them. Immediately after that, two more voices came over, saying, "Stop hurting us." I knew they weren't talking to us, as we'd just explained we were not about that. Were they speaking of past investigators? Or was there something sinister going on within the spirit realm of Bobby Mackey's?

Clayton then asked Abby, "Is there someone here

hurting you?" And we got no response. It felt like the spirit who went by Abby was no longer with us, and Clayton and I both started feeling light-headed at the exact same time. Was Abby pulling energy from us to manifest again? Or was a more sinister spirit here with us now? Regardless, neither one of us liked the way it was making us feel.

As we were discussing what could be causing our dizzy spells, suddenly Clayton heard the sound of pants swishing. It was definitely not Abby in here with us anymore. We turned the Odd Box off for a bit and just listened to see if we could hear it again, and sadly we heard nothing else. But then, out of the blue, I felt a tug on my arm, and my crazy was telling me to go down-stairs to investigate next. I followed my instinct, and the crew and I started packing up our equipment to head down into the honky-tonk area of the building.

We headed downstairs into a large open room with pool tables and some video games on the far wall, and the main bar just opposite. There are several tables throughout this massive room, and a mechanical bull in the center. I wanted to ride that thing so bad, but this forty-something-year-old body would probably end up paralyzed.

We brought all of our equipment over to the far wall and set things up on and around the three pool tables. We'd brought to this investigation our SLS, or stick-figure camera, our dowsing rods, a flashlight, and of course the Odd Box. Clayton was settled in his spot as I turned the SLS camera on, and the moment things were rolling, I noticed a stick figure in the area where Clayton was sitting, but it was not mapping Clayton. The stick figure mapped was above Clayton, and while Clayton was sitting still, this stick figure was almost vibrating, or just had far too many espresso shots in the old iced latte this evening.

I tried speaking to the anomaly, to see if it would mimic my commands like raising a hand, or moving one of its legs, but it stayed in the same position, looking like it was shivering. I then walked closer to where the stick figure was, to try to judge the distance. And we concluded it was in front of Clayton, and the camera was still not recognizing Clayton at all. It just stayed there until after a few solid minutes, it disappeared. However, the camera still didn't recognize Clayton, very odd indeed.

We got back to the investigation, and I introduced everyone, as I always do, and let any spirits who might be in this massive room know our intentions. I also said to any ghosts that might be in earshot, we knew the stories that came from the other groups who investigated here, and I didn't feel the evil demonic vibe at all. I asked Clayton if he felt anything bad, and his response was, "Not yet." To which I replied, "I feel if this place was as evil as everyone says it is, we would feel it everywhere." And Clayton agreed.

I'm going to go into another theory of mine here, she says as she steps up onto her high horse. I feel if you go in expecting demons, or evil, you're gonna be looking for it. If anything feels off while investigating, your mind will go directly to the worst-case scenario. I go in with a totally open mind. I'm aware of the legends of the place we're investigating, but I'm not searching for that same experience others have at the site. I want to experience what I am supposed to experience. No preconceived notions and an open mind are what make our investigations so eventful. We're open to whoever wants to speak to us and tell their story. I was a little uneasy going into this place, but I had to shake it off and reset my mind before the investigation started. And that was exactly what I did, and it sure as hell worked upstairs, so I was gonna continue doing what I do and hope for the best.

Clayton then shouted, "Something touched my stool!" He stayed put but was repeating over and over again that something had touched his stool. He was sitting at a high-top table on a barstool. We all remained calmish. And he explained exactly what he had felt: "Like I felt the whole stool move." I processed this for a moment. I knew he was more on edge than I was, and I didn't want him to lose his shit this early in the investigation. I did what we do when someone starts feeling uneasy, I recited, "We're not here to hurt you are harm you, yell at you, or bully you in any way. We're just here to find out more about you." And then I told Clayton what it was my "crazy" was telling me. I was feeling the sense that the spirits were just checking us out, to see if we are who we say we are. And I told him that maybe whatever it was that moved his stool was just trying to get a reaction out of him. And staying calm was what we needed to do.

Both of us then felt a heat sensation at the same time. Clayton felt it on his shoulder and described it like a lighter was lit near it, and I described what I felt: it was like two very hot hands grabbing me on the inside of my elbow. But we both remained calm. I literally think, looking back, the spirits were testing us. Trying to get a rise out of us. Similar to the way things had happened at Fear Factory. Because that was what was expected of them. But our staying calm showed them we weren't going to react the way they thought we would.

I was ready to go on with the investigation, and I pulled out the dowsing rods. I let them know I would like to communicate through these right now, and to cross the rods into an X for a yes answer and don't do anything if the answer is no. And I asked if there were any other people here besides myself, Clayton, Carter and James. And I asked if there was someone who could come up and cross the rods in my hand. And after quite a bit of coaxing, the rods finally crossed. It was GAME ON.

I asked if the entity I was speaking with was a female,

or a girl, and the rods crossed almost immediately. I then asked this spirit to uncross them. I do this to show myself that they are still here and interacting with us. And the rods uncrossed. I wasn't feeling any pulling on the rods like I sometimes do; it was just a fluid swing.

The next question I asked was, "Are you Abby from upstairs?" It took a beat for the rods to start crossing again, but as they did, I got a pain in my stomach. Not a sharp pain, but like something had reached in and was squeezing my actual stomach. I couldn't double over in pain at that point, because the communication was just getting good. If I move, the rods move. And now we knew we were communicating directly with the spirit I had just seen upstairs. And now I felt the pulling on the rods like I had so many times before. And I was hoping that our connection with her was even stronger now. And I also noticed that the pain in my stomach had subsided just as quickly as it came on.

Clayton asked us all, "Didn't anyone hear that?" And we hadn't, so we asked what he had heard, and he told us that he'd just heard a female giggle right in between him and me, which was less than four feet between us. I wish I knew the reason some people hear things that others don't. But this was why I was here, what I was trying to figure out. This was one of the about three million questions I have about hauntings. But there was no time to dwell in the moment. I needed to ask, "Abby, was that you my friend Clayton just heard?" Without hesitation, the rods crossed immediately.

Clayton, still slightly dumbfounded, asked Abby to show herself to us, and even though I didn't think he was asking specifically for the dowsing rods, the rods crossed the quickest they had yet. Clayton again, this time to the room in general, said, "Abby, please show yourself to us in any form." And I then asked specifically, "Abby, please point the rods to where we will see you." And the rods just uncrossed. She was at that point not willing to show herself to any other members of the crew yet.

Clayton continued to talk to her and told her he knew she was there, and that we weren't there to exploit her, that we just wanted to hear her story, and the rods crossed. As if she was saying she knew all of this and was comfortable with us. In my heart of hearts sitting there on a pool table in Northern Kentucky, I thought that was why she showed herself to me in the first place. Clayton continued to assure her we weren't there for anything else but her story. And as he was speaking to her, he stopped abruptly and clicked on his flashlight and pointed it at the floor just behind the pool table I was sitting on, and said, "What the fuck was that?" We were all just staring at him, and he said, "I just saw a glow!" pointing to the opposite side of the pool table from where I was. And he exclaimed he'd seen a glow moving on the floor.

Now we had no flashlights on. Our cameras were emitting a light that the human eye cannot even see. So we knew for a fact that glow didn't come from any of us. There are zero windows in this section of the location, so what he saw was absolutely paranormal. Since what I saw was a glowing ball of light, this meant to me that this glow Clayton saw was Abby showing herself to him, just like he was asking her to. I believed every word he was saying, and I thought we were the lucky two she decided to show herself to. And Abby confirmed this herself when I asked her if Clayton had just seen her, and the dowsing rods crossed immediately to an X.

Now it was time to find out more about this young lady who had so much to say to us this evening. I asked her if she was under the age of twenty-five. My crazy was telling me between nineteen and twenty. Just then Clayton got up because he was seeing a void of light where he could previously see one coming out of the gift shop, where we had all of our equipment.

As he and the boys went to check it out, I tried to keep the line of communication open with our new friend Abby. I next asked her if she could point the dowsing rods in the direction of the area we should investigate next, and as the boys were trying without success to debunk what Clayton was seeing, there were several loud knocks on one of the pool tables. I was now by myself in this area. I visibly jumped, put on my mommy voice, and demanded to know who was over here. I could plainly see the boys, they were about twenty-five yards away from me, so I knew for a fact it wasn't them. It was not a firework from outside, it was a succession of knocks not ten feet away from me. My camera clearly picked it up as well. Even the boys, being so far away, all heard it. And upon replay of the camera audio, it sounds like pool balls being bounced around on one of the pool tables; however, none of the pool balls were on any of the tables.

So the boys came back, and I re-asked the question to Abby and reworded it a little bit. I asked, "Can you point these rods in the direction where we should go after we're done talking to you?" And one of the rods stayed completely still, and the other pointed directly to where the boys just were. I mean, she had a point; it seemed pretty active over there. And then Carter AND James both saw what Clayton had seen earlier, a void of light pass in front of the static light from left to right. At that point I was the only one who hadn't seen it, since I had been so focused on communicating with Abby. And since she had just told us that this was where we should be investigating, I set down the dowsing rods for a moment and stared intently at what everyone was seeing but me.

And then I saw it too. It was like a shadow or void of light walking from left to right, over and over and over again. I picked up the dowsing rods one last time and asked, "Hey, Abby, should we go over there now?" And the rods crossed immediately, almost with an urgency. And then the knocking started again, but this time, it was coming from the gift shop area. Someone was sure trying to get our attention. Unfortunately none of these shadows were captured with our cameras, it was only visible to the human eye, but the fact that each of us saw it was enough evidence for me.

During the distanced investigation of the hallway, my camera died, with three hours of recording battery left, and then all the other cameras slowly drained out. And again, I was taking this as a good sign, that the spirits were utilizing any energy they could find to keep communicating with us. Were they trying to distract us to pull the energy from our equipment? Was that why the sudden activity in the hallways began? Only time would tell. But two different areas in the same location were as active as we had hoped they'd be and then some.

We thanked them for their cooperation and headed to get our batteries swapped out, and decided where we would investigate next. We were in the gift shop area, and no activity happened anywhere near where we were, when just minutes ago it was like the spiritual honky-tonk was open for business just feet from where we currently were. Mind-boggling was the only explanation I had for it.

We decided our next stop would be the basement, the basement where the well to hell is said to be. And I got the bright idea to go in blindfolded. But not to just be a badass or anything like that, it was more so I could tune into my senses as I entered and get a feel for the place through feelings, or my "crazy" as I like to call it. I was afraid going in and seeing the same basement I had seen on just about every paranormal investigative show on cable, I would let my preconceived notions get in the way. I put on a blindfold and made everyone promise me that they wouldn't drop me down the alleged well to hell, and I let them find a place to put me, and we'd go from there.

Did they leave me alone in what is considered one of the most demon-infested places in the country? YEP, they sure did. But I wasn't scared. I didn't even feel uneasy. As I stayed there with my blindfold on, and my camera accidentally recording upside down, I felt fine, even a sense of peace. I'm not saying that there's nothing there. But there was no overwhelming feeling of ANYTHING in the basement of Bobby Mackey's. And that was a huge relief. Now I'm not saying horrible things haven't happened down there. I don't know, I wasn't there when these things happened, but remember, you get what you put out. And there I was putting out all the love, light, peace, and positivity I could. And there I was in the dead center of this allegedly demon-infested basement and not scared at all. Until I couldn't hear the boys anymore. Then I gave them a holler, mostly out of boredom, but if I started thinking too hard about being there by myself, I might start reminiscing about the "best of the paranormal cable demon brigade" in my head. So Clayton came and grabbed me to lead me to what they decided was the cell, and that was all I knew.

I walked through clumsily, and it wasn't a far walk, but I was sat in another location that I knew absolutely nothing about. Carter noticed that I'd been filming upside down the entire time, and as he was telling me this, I heard a male voice off in the distance, but it was too far away for me to make out what was said. And Clayton mentioned he'd heard movement upstairs, which was later debunked as the tour guide (who was waiting out in her car while we investigated and went in for a moment). We captured a flashlight on one of our GoPros.

I heard a male voice again, and it sounded again like they were very far behind me, yelling. So I asked the boys one question about my location, "Is there a wall behind me?" And Carter then told me that I had a solid concrete wall behind me. Super weird, because on the other side of that concrete wall is dirt, or earth, whatever you want to call it. There are no living people back there.

So then we set up for me to do the Estes method. We don't do this very often, and I'm not sure why. This was our second time trying it, and the first time was very successful. How this works is you plug the spirit box into noise-canceling headphones instead of the Odd

Box or a regular speaker. And we have another of us asking questions, either in a different room, or in this case I was blindfolded so I couldn't cheat and see Clayton and figure out what he was saying via reading his lips. And at this moment, after Clayton got the spirit box running in my headphones, he would start asking questions to any spirits near us, and I would say out loud and repeat what any discernible voices said that I heard in my headphones.

As Clayton let any entities in the area know we've come out of love, light, peace, and positivity, etc., he also stated that we knew what this basement was known for (demons and more demons), but we personally knew there was more to this space. As he was saying this, I felt a hand being placed on my right shoulder. And I was going to take this as a good sign. While I didn't know what Clayton was saying, it wasn't a scary touch at all, it almost felt comforting. I asked the boys overly loudly, because I had the spirit box blasting directly into my eardrums, if it was one of them, to which I got a resounding no. I responded, again a little too loudly, COOL.

Clayton then began his questioning, "Can you please tell Kitsie how many of you are down here?" To which I said immediately, "Jesus." OK, not quite the response we were expecting for this allegedly evil basement, but at least it wasn't spewing out words like demon and devil.

Clayton then asked, "What is your last name?" To

which I responded, "Edward or Edwan." And then "Ed" came over twice in a row, and yet again the name Edward was said again. As you would imagine, we decided to call this entity Ed. Then Clayton only addressed Ed by saying his name, and I said out loud right after Ed was addressed and nothing more that I heard the word "true," actually affirming this was who we were speaking to. Clayton then asked, "Ed, how many people are down here with you?" To which I immediately heard and then said, "Five." Now again, I can't stress enough that I could not hear Clayton at all, I had a blindfold on, and he was turned away from me just to make sure.

Then with nothing asked by Clayton, I heard, "You're swell," and repeated it to the room. Awwww, what a great demonless start we had down in the basement, and the spirits seemed to like us. Clayton then asked if it bothered Ed that so many people came down here to try to speak to him. To which I heard no answer coming through the spirit box to my ears. Clayton then asked if Ed could repeat one of our names, to which I responded immediately, "Clayton," after hearing it in my headphones.

Clayton then said, "Ed, we just want to learn about you so that we can tell your story." To which I replied, after hearing it come through my headphones, "Be kind." Wow, this is a theme in locations that are known for demonic spirit activity. The spirits at this location just want kindness. Which is exactly what we intend to keep showing them. I wanted the stories from this place that no one else had gotten before, and I thought this was exactly what was happening.

Just before Clayton could ask the next question, I felt the sensation of two fingers gently stroking my back from my neck down to my waist. And it tickled and freaked me out a little at the same time. I might or might not have overreacted a little because my back was leaning up against the back of the chair at the time, and there was no way a human could have done that. But I settled myself back down quickly so we could continue. And a child's voice came through the headphones, saying, "Stay." Clayton then asked out loud, "What is the child's name?" to which I replied what I heard immediately, "Timothy."

Suddenly, Clayton was distracted by a noise in the other room, and I said with zero prompting, "Please stop him now." And then Clayton heard what he thought was Carter clearing his throat. But when he asked Carter if he did, he replied, "I did not." And out of the blue again, I said, "Please." Clayton was in the process of freaking out. Was the child talking about Clayton? Did I need to calm him down? Or was the child referring to the noises Clayton was hearing as "him"?

We found out pretty quickly that Clayton's instincts were dead-on. As Clayton asked whoever was speaking to me what the noise was, I responded, "Get rid of it," after hearing the spirit box say the exact same thing. Then Clayton specifically asked, "What made that growling sound?" And he got no response. Clayton then decided it was time to tell me what was going on.

As I took my blindfold off, I realized I was in a mini caged-off area, with a compressor on one side with lots of plumbing pipes, a table on the other side covered in workman's type stuff, and just like Carter said, a concrete wall behind me. In front of me, just beyond what I would have to say was chicken wire from floor to ceiling except for a small doorway out of this area, was a large room, with a couch, a coffee table, and a shelving unit on the opposite wall. And a doorway to leave the room. On the shelves were several items set up like a storage area. Then Clayton told me about the growl he'd heard, and I could tell he was shaken. So we discussed what had just happened, and I had no answers.

We decided it was time for Clayton to put on the headphones, and I'd ask the questions and deal with whatever was growling. The last time we did this, we each had totally different experiences in the same location. So it was time to see if this would happen again, and as he was putting on the headphones, I clearly heard a child say an entire sentence. I asked Clayton if he heard it, and what he heard was a child saying, "Please forgive me." Clayton finished putting on the headphones and told us his true feelings, "I already hate this." But he did it anyway, even though he was completely on edge.

I left Clayton in the chicken-wire cage and headed out to the main room. Since Clayton didn't want to wear the blindfold, I turned completely away from him to start asking my questions. My first question was blunt and to the point. "Who growled, really, seriously?" To which there was no response. So I continued, "We're not here to mess with you. I know you're trying to scare us, and I don't have time for that shit. Tell me more about yourself." To which the response was puzzling, "He's running." I asked who was running, and then Clayton, speaking for the spirits, said, "Me." I couldn't shake the feeling that this spirit was trying to tell me something, but it was coming over like a puzzle that I just couldn't decipher. At this point, I was sick of playing games, and I wanted to put my crew at ease, so I asked straight up, "So, are there demons down here?" To which Clayton relayed the message he'd just heard, "You're safe." Still not the direct answer I was looking for, but maybe my crew would now be a little more at ease.

Carter actually said, "Well, that's actually the only question I wanted the answer to." So mission accomplished there. The crew was more at ease, and I think Clayton hearing "you're safe" even before we did put him at ease as well.

So let's get back to the storytelling. I asked, "Are there spirits down here?" To which Clayton said, "Yep." Then I asked, "Who's the little girl I heard?" and immediately Clayton gave me the response given to him and said, "Ann," out loud in a singsongy voice, which was just how he had heard it. I kept trying to find out more about my new friend Ann. I asked her how old she was, and Clayton, responding for her, said, "Twelve." WHOA, these answers were coming just as quickly as a real-time conversation would. The only delay was me coming up with the next question.

Clayton then, just out of the blue, said, "Dead." It was always reassuring when the entities know they are dead, we never assume they know, and I certainly don't want to be the one to break the news to them as a conversation starter. So that was out of the way.

I then asked, "How many other spirits are down here with us?" To which Clayton responded in a quiet voice, again mimicking how he was hearing the response, "Many." And there it was. I was a little intimidated at that point. I was expecting, like, a five or a six. YIKES.

I asked, "Can you tell me the names of the others, Ann?" And immediately Clayton said, "Which one?" I then asked, "Can you see them?" And she responded to Clayton, "All of them."

I then asked Ann, "How many of us are here with you that aren't normally here?" And he then responded, "Four." Which was actually the first time we'd gotten this response. Usually we get responses of a plus one to however many are in our group, and I just usually assume it's Anna, the spirit from Culbertson mansion that followed me home. Maybe she didn't want to go along on this trip, or maybe she just stayed upstairs. We never really do know unless she comes across on a spirit box session of some sort, which she does quite often, always with the same voice.

Then Clayton felt a pinch of some sort on his back and jumped, and then the pièce de résistance of the alleged demon basement happened. We were all feeling pretty comfortable at this point. I mean, we'd literally been told we were safe. James and Carter and I were waiting for Clayton to tell us what was going on with his back. And remember that compressor that was right next to the chair I was sitting in? Well, Clayton was next to it right now, and it went off, did its thing, which I was assuming was on a timer of some sort for the moment, and it was the loudest, most obnoxious sound I'd ever heard. Clayton jumped, I screamed, and we were all just completely thrown off guard. Carter ran in and flipped the on switch off to turn it off. And two seconds later we were all laughing uncontrollably for the next two minutes. Finally Clayton said, "How did that thing turn on?" and Carter had the best response to anything that entire night. He said, "It was probably a goddamned ghost!" So you guessed it, we laughed a whole lot more.

I've looked over the footage, and I don't see anything being switched on or off, on the compressor, and Carter actually had to switch it off to turn it off. We even asked our tour guide for the night if it was on a timer, and she said no, and she went on to say it's never gone off with someone in the room. But the fact that Clayton felt something touch him not even seconds before the thing turned on, and Carter had to go in and flip a switch to off tells us all that it was actually turned on by something unseen. Ghosts 1, Oddity Files Crew 0.

Clayton decided to go back under and get more answers. We were hoping all of the commotion didn't scare our new friend Ann off. I just got back into asking questions, and asked, "Ann, who's here with you?" To which Clayton's immediate response was, "Child." And we were back in business, baby. I asked her how many children, to which the immediate response was, "Ten." Then Clayton said, "Hold." And we thought nothing of it until I felt something tugging on the wireless microphone pack attached to the back of my jeans. Clayton said again, "Hold." Was one of these ten children trying to hold on to me? My mind was so blown away at how relevant each and every answer was from the child named Ann. I then asked her, "Can you go and touch Clayton for me?" And she immediately responded through Clayton, "Germs." I mean, what a kid's thing to say, she just told me she didn't want to touch Clayton because he has cooties. How hilariously adorable.

I then asked Ann to tell me her friends' names, to which she responded, "They… are here," with a distinct pause between *they* and *are*. And then I asked her where we should go next, or if she'd like us to stay and talk to her, and her response was so sweet. Clayton, responding for this chatty little girl, said, "So long." I asked again where should we go next, and Clayton, responding again for Ann, said, "Warning." To which I responded, "Warning from what, honey?" And she responded rather cryptically, "That boy." I then asked, "What boy? And her response was, "That corner." Her warning didn't make sense at the time, but we were hoping it would later.

We made our way back to the main building upstairs and decided all of us but Clayton were going to check out the area of the building where the stage is. Clayton would be heading into the men's restroom for a solo investigation. This corner bathroom had a lot of hype around it as well. And Clayton wanted to see what all the hubbub was all about.

So Carter, James and I sat down in some seats out by the stage, and after taking bets of how long we thought Clayton would last in the bathroom by himself, we just kind of gave a listen to see what we could hear, hoping for whispers or footsteps, and especially the shadow people that are said to be there. Listening intently, BINGO, Carter heard a shuffle and then saw a shadow from the corner of his eye, heading Clayton's way, and just seconds later we heard Clayton yell out to us, "Where are you guys at?" then, "Did one of you guys just walk by?" To which I replied, "No, but Carter just saw something coming your way." And that was when Clayton came to us to tell us about his experience. He told us he had heard footsteps right outside the corner men's room just before yelling out to us. Carter then explained what he saw and heard and walked it out to time it. He discovered, for the same thing he saw to walk by where Clayton heard the same thing, it was right on pace to have made it there when Clayton heard it. Pretty cool, right, but where did it go, who was it, and was it residual or intelligent?

We decided to continue to try to get some evidence of this mysterious shadow. Clayton went back in the bathroom and left the flashlight on this time, and I can't say I blame him. He heard footsteps walking down the hallway to the restrooms, which stopped right before going in to the men's room he was standing in. While the footsteps he'd heard earlier were on a hard surface, just like Carter heard, this time he heard feet on a carpet. The hallway that led to the bathroom from the bar area was covered in carpet. Things were getting pretty real for Clayton, and then he heard a female whisper outside the men's room's open doorway. I was a million percent sure it wasn't me; we had gone back into the large room with the mechanical bull, where we'd had the dowsing rod session, which probably a hundred yards away. So he asked me to go in and see if I got any feelings or spidey tingles in there.

I wanted to hear footsteps and hear whispers, so I walked in, but respectfully announced there was a lady in the house, and the moment I walked in, I felt a fear, but not my fear, like someone else who was in here was terrified. And just a gross feeling in this room, not evil, not good, just gross (and yes, the bathroom was clean). I walked out and announced, "I don't like it in here. I don't like it at all. I feel a fear, but I'm not scared. It's like I'm feeling someone else's fear."

Clayton asked me just to stay in for a full sixty seconds. And I mean, it was the least I could do; he had been in there much longer. I walked back in and stayed half inside and half outside the open door. Then it happened, I had a memory that wasn't mine flash through my head, similar to what had happened to me at Culbertson, and when it did, it was like I was in the moment, a moment a very long time ago. The fear that felt like someone else's earlier was now mine, and then I saw in my mind's eye, a scuffle of a male and a female, but I was the woman, and that woman was being raped by a large sweaty man with greasy hair, with her face mashed up against the wall, and she could see him out of the corner of her eye. But I wasn't mashed up against a wall, I was standing right in the doorway because I didn't have time to enter fully before this "vision," for lack of a better word, came over me. But was this the man in the corner whom Ann was warning us about downstairs?

I had only had something like this happen to me two other times. The first was after my first time investigating the Old Lake County Jail and Sherriff's House.

And it was the same thing, a memory that wasn't mine played out in my head, but this time I was an onlooker to a male lifting up a woman by the neck against a wall and screaming at her. The couple was dressed in formal attire and appeared to be in early twentieth-century clothing. But that was it. Now what I can say is that that these women were in danger; maybe that's what it takes for me to have this happen. I too was in a violent relationship in the past, and I found my way out of it. Maybe they show this to me because they know I will understand. This is still to this day something I am still trying to process.

I walked back out after about forty-five seconds and told the crew what I had just been a kind of a witness to. I explained to them the instance at Lake County, which I had never told them about before. I told them that the men's room just felt so very angry now. But we were done in there; there was no need to go back. I know now why I was shown this horrific scene, and you're about to find out too. But it was very residual, and there are no spirits that will rape you in the men's room at Bobby Mackey's. But that energy, that moment was left behind, and it's a nasty anger that I wish no one else to ever feel again.

We decided to move on back to where the performance stage is, and brought Clayton with us this time. I set up the Odd Box, because we hadn't used it since we were upstairs at the beginning of the evening. We all knew so much more now, and I personally had to get the full story. Most importantly I needed to know whose memory that was. My first thought was Abby, because she was the entity we'd had the most contact with this evening, but I couldn't be sure. But the Odd Box was the perfect way to find out. Things were set up, and we got ready to start with some questions.

Just before we started, there was a loud noise on the opposite side of the bar. But I'd learned over the years not to chase after the noises, to let the noises come to me. So we just continued. Clayton asked the box, "Who was walking around outside the bathroom?" And very quickly, a female voice came through the box, saying, "I did."

He phrased the question a little differently since we had the doorway to communication open. He asked, "Was that you by the bathroom?" And the female voice came over again and said, "Yes."

And I burst in with the question of the hour, I asked, "What happened to you in that bathroom? We're not going to judge you. We KNOW it's not your fault." Clayton then added, "He can't hurt you anymore." And as I was reassuring her I would protect her, she came over the Odd Box and said, "He hurt me." But a male voice came over immediately after her response and said, "Rape." Moments later the same male voice came over and said, "Lies," and after that the female voice came over twice, but what she was saying was indecipherable. The male voice came over and said, "Abby."

That was when we got a little overprotective. And Clayton pulled out the daddy voice for the first time ever. And he told Abby that this male voice we were hearing and so leery of could not do anything to hurt her anymore. He went on to say, "You need to let her speak." And I chimed in right after with, "You need to fuck right off is what you need to do."

The male voice then said, "Bobby."

Other than that one name, we got silence for a few moments, and I thought we had lost her. I came in again and said sternly but not rudely, "Sir, you need to back off and let her tell her story. You can tell us your story when she's done, but right now, I want to hear her story. Abby, is that you?" And holy hell, it worked. When I told him to fuck off, we got nothing, but when I explained what I actually wanted, he let her speak, and Abby verified with a loud and clear, "YES," after I asked, "Abby, is that you?" that it was her we were speaking to, and by doing that verified to me it was her memory I had witnessed in the bathroom. I realized then this night was all about Abby.

I thanked Clayton for making me go in the bathroom when I didn't want to; otherwise I wouldn't know her story. Clayton was trying to figure out who was outside the bathroom and asked if it was Abby. I said to him, "I feel like she would be anywhere here BUT that bathroom." And her voice came over and said, "Killed him." Wait, what? Were they both stuck here because of that one incident, and that incident ended in a murder?

I asked her why she was here, and got no answer. I asked if she was here to tell this story, and a very LOUD voice came over and said, "YES." I then went on to tell her maybe now she could move on. I told her she didn't have to keep reliving this awful memory, that she didn't have to stay here. And several minutes went by without another response from Abby.

So Clayton asked if there was anyone else who would like to talk, and a very deep voice came over and to me sounded like "Stephen," but Carter and Clayton swear they heard "demon." I just ignored it and moved on, but there was nothing else to move on to. The Odd Box was silent.

James then chimed in with the question of the night, "Who did this to you?" And when she spoke again for the first time in a while, none of us could agree on what she said. It was like the line of communication was getting stretched too thin or something. And with as much activity as we'd had, I was sure they were running low on energy, and I knew we were. Clayton heard *Bob*, Carter heard *John*, and I thought I heard *a cop*. Man of the hour James then asked, "What letter did his name start with?" This kid is a genius. And immediately Abby's voice said, "B," and the name Bobby had come over earlier. Maybe it wasn't referring to Bobby Mackey.

There are a whole hell of a lot of other Bobbys out in the world.

And my next question confirmed this, I asked her, "Was the name of the man who hurt you Bobby?" And immediately she came over and said, "It was." WOW, I wasn't asking the right questions anymore, but I felt like we were back on track again; thanks, James, for the assist. Sometimes when we have so much communication with one spirit, this is gonna sound cuckoo, but I feel like they should be able to tell me anything. I forget we have to be the ones to keep the conversation on the right track; the Wonder Box isn't just going to blurt out an entire monologue on exactly what is happening.

I asked her, "Was there more than one?" Meaning was she the only woman that this happened to, or were there more. And a barrage of other voices just came in out of the blue. A voice saying, "Can you see us?" And a different voice saying, "Hazel?" And the word eleven came over several times in different voices. And because it wasn't Abby's voice, I discounted it at the time. But typing this out right now, was it the women who had been raped asking if we saw them? Was Hazel another of Bobby with no last name's victims? Were there eleven victims total? Hindsight is always twenty-twenty, isn't it?

We decided to make one more quick move to the back of the stage area and do a quick Odd Box session back there. Clayton told me this was where Carl had

had his exorcism back in the day. Clayton asked right off the bat, "Carl, are you here?" And what sounded like three or four people talking at once responded, "He's gone." To which Clayton questioned, "Where did he go?" And a strong male voice came over and said, "HOME." Which honestly could mean so many different things. It could mean Heaven, it could mean back upstairs where he lived, or maybe some other home where he had lived. But I'll leave that up to your interpretation.

I tried one more time to talk to Abby, and I asked her if she was still with us, to which she responded almost immediately, "Yeah, I'm dead." She took a brief pause and said, "I killed him." But not in a voice of regret, but almost in a matter-of-fact kind of way.

She then continued to tell us that she, "Hit him." And then was when I realized we had fifteen minutes to pack up and be out of this place for this night. I thanked Abby and anyone who communicated with us for their time, and loud and clear a child's voice came over, sounding just like one of the kids from the *Little Rascals*, and said, "Good people." Talk about the best compliment coming from the spirit realm.

And on a parting note, we let the spirits know we were sorry that so many people went there and harassed them. And Clayton made sure the spirits were aware that they could not follow us home or attach themselves to our equipment in any way, shape, or form. And a female voice beamed over the Odd Box, saying, "We know."

And that was our first and only investigation of Bobby Mackey's Music World. We dealt with no evil, no demons; we had laughs, screams, and confessions of murder. I would say it was one hell of an investigation (pun intended). I can't believe the luck we had there. I believe both Clayton and I saw a piece of Abby that night, and all four of us were blown away by her communication.

We packed up and headed to our cars. I lit up some sage, and we asked for protection against any spirits following us home, surrounded ourselves with love, light, peace, and positivity, and headed our separate ways.

That was the last episode we needed for our season 3 on Prime Video, and what a way to round out a season where we visited Octagon Hall, Mitchell Opera House, Fear Factory, and Waverly Hills Sanatorium.

CONCLUSION

We didn't investigate again for over seven months. When we finally did, we headed out to Virginia Beach, Virginia, and I was finally able to show Carter and Clayton Ferry Plantation. This is the location where I saw my first ghost apparition! It was still as beautiful as I remembered, and I was so excited to introduce Carter and Clayton to the spirits, who are all still there. But the reaction wasn't what I expected at first. They were almost standoffish. And we found out why. Without writing a whole new chapter on an episode that hasn't been edited yet, I'll give you the CliffsNotes version. The resident spirits were upset that I had brought another spirit with me that they weren't familiar with. And it wasn't Anna. Apparently for the past seven months, Abby from Bobby Mackey's had been following me around in stealth mode.

The gentleman who had to stay at the location and gave us the tour is an empath. And he saw the spirit that I brought with me. She was around twenty years old, with dirty dishwater hair in a short bob like the girls would wear in the '20s and '30s, and was an average height. And as soon as Cody described her to me, I knew who it was. It was Abby. The two spirits that I bonded with so closely felt the need to stay with me. Even though I'd smudged when I left Bobby Mackey's, she'd found a way to do so. I've never understood why if you tell a spirit they can't follow you home, they have to listen to any of us. And now I know they don't have to. I think it's just peace of mind that paranormal investigators tell themselves to keep them at ease.

But again, like Anna, I told her to follow me downstairs, I told her I would protect her, and why would she want to be somewhere she has such horrible memories?

The next investigation, and the last one we've done to date, was just Carter and me. We were at Randolph County Asylum in Winchester, Indiana. I again won't go into extreme detail about the full investigation. But when we started our investigation, both Anna and Abby chose to tell me why they are still with me to this day. Anna told us, via a dowsing rod session, that she and Abby are with us, and they are there to help the spirits know we mean no harm to them, and to encourage other spirits to communicate with me and my crew. I hadn't really thought about it, but Anna had been quiet in the house as of late, but I'm pretty sure now that she and Abby are together, they are able to entertain each other, and I'm OK with this.

I thank both of them for their help and appreciate that they chose me to help out.

Kitsie Duncan has been investigating the paranormal for twelve years. She's the producer and lead investigator for the TV series *Oddity Files* on Amazon Prime, the co-host of *Oddity Files* the podcast and the true crime podcast *Miss Murder*, and hosts the *Get Scared* podcast.

Kitsie investigates differently than most. She goes in with love, light, peace and positivity and helps the spirits tell their stories.

Visit her: https://www.flow.page/kitsieduncan

facebook.com/kitsieduncanofficial
twitter.com/Kitsieduncan
instagram.com/Kitsieduncan